THE GOSPEL CALL AND CONVERSION THEOLOGY OF JAMES

Curtis Braun

New Harbor Press

Copyright © 2022 Curtis Braun

All rights reserved. No part of this publication may be reproduced, distributed or transmitted in any form or by any means, including photocopying, recording, or other electronic or mechanical methods, without the prior written permission of the publisher, except in the case of brief quotations embodied in critical reviews and certain other non-commercial uses permitted by copyright law. For permission requests, write to the publisher, addressed "Attention: Permissions Coordinator," at the address below.

New Harbor Press
1601 Mt Rushmore Rd, Ste 3288
Rapid City, SD 57701
www.newharborpress.com

Ordering Information:
Quantity sales. Special discounts are available on quantity purchases by corporations, associations, and others. For details, contact the "Special Sales Department" at the address above.

The Gospel Call and Conversion Theology of James/Braun —1st ed.

ISBN 978-1-63357-292-8

First editon: 10 9 8 7 6 5 4 3 2 1

Contents

Preface 1

Acknowledgments 5

Dedication and Prayer 7

Introduction 9

Chapter 1: The Gospel Call for Submissive and Obedient Faith toward the Lord Jesus Christ 15

Chapter 2: The Gospel Call for Preeminent Loving Faith toward the Lord Jesus Christ 41

Chapter 3: The Gospel Call for Repentant Faith: Turning Away from Sin and toward the Lord Jesus Christ 67

Chapter 4: The Gospel Call for Repentant Faith: Godly Sorrow for Sin against God 93

Chapter 5: The Gospel Call for a Humble Faith toward the Lord Jesus Christ 119

Chapter 6: James: Let Not Many Become Teachers 163

Bibliography 181

Preface

There has been a great burden placed on me to continue to defend and proclaim the gospel. Much of what I have written has been to address sacramentalism that is associated with Christianity. The first book I wrote, *The False Gospel of Baptismal Regeneration in the Lutheran Church and Christ's Call to Saving Faith*, was written to address the conservative Lutheran Church and address the false gospel they were proclaiming and defending. It was the church and denomination that I was raised in, and it is where many of my family and friends remain. Therefore, my burden was to write and address this gospel issue. In this book, I sought to address the specific doctrinal issue of baptismal regeneration by separating and distinguishing water baptism and baptism with the Holy Spirit. I also sought to explain how baptismal regeneration corrupted, twisted, and destroyed the doctrines of regeneration, conversion, and baptism with the Holy Spirit. Most importantly, this book was written to exegetically explain how baptismal regeneration is a condemning false gospel which clashes with the true gospel of the Lord Jesus Christ.

The second book I wrote, *The Gospel—The Biblical Means to Identify False Teachers and False Gospels*, was written to present and help define the true gospel, identify the essential components of the gospel, identify a false teacher, and define how to deal with false teachers. I saw that there was a need to define the gospel to identify false gospels and false teachers. I also saw there was very little discernment or warnings within Christianity which gave biblical criteria on what qualifies an individual as a false teacher. This was my motivation for writing the second book.

The third book I wrote, *The Apostle Paul's Theology on Conversion and Condemnation of Sacramental Conversion*, was written to exegetically demonstrate the apostle Paul's understanding and theology on conversion (e.g., repentance and faith in Jesus Christ) as well as display his utter rejection and denunciation of sacramental conversion. The apostle Paul was and is often proof texted as one teaching conversion, regeneration, and salvation by sacraments, but there is no consideration given to Paul's preconversion life as a ritualistic and ceremonial Pharisee. It is troublesome to see how Paul's letters and teaching in Scripture can be twisted in such a way that portray the apostle Paul as teaching sacramental conversion. In this book, I attempted to show how Paul would have put no hope for salvation in circumcision or covenant signs, ceremonial and external washings, Sabbath observances or law keeping, and burnt offerings and sacrifices. The goal was to show that Paul responded to, taught, and proclaimed the reconciling gospel call of repentance toward God and faith in the Lord Jesus Christ. Lastly, I set out to show that Paul was aggressive in defending the gospel against false teachers and false gospels and demonstrate that Paul's stand against such false teachers was simply him imitating Christ (1 Corinthians 11:1).

In this fourth book, I am specifically highlighting the gospel call that James gives in James 4:7–10. In these four verses, James will give ten aorist imperatives that capture the nature of saving faith and conversion. I will exposit these ten aorist commands given by James and explain how these commands are a gospel invitation to come to and follow Christ in a salvific way. I will also demonstrate that the gospel call that James issues is greatly influenced by the gospel calls and teaching of the Lord Jesus Christ. Lastly, I will demonstrate that James, the half-brother of Jesus, was very concerned about false teaching, false gospels, and gave a stern command and warning to those considering the position of teaching and leading in the church.

Also, this fourth book is written to bring awareness of churches that teach sacramental conversion, and thus, give a false gospel and false assurance of one's salvation. In the books I have written, I've always attempted to replace false doctrine with true doctrine. For example, in my first book I sought to explain true regeneration which exposed baptismal regeneration as false. In the second book, I sought to explain the true gospel which would expose a false gospel. In the third book, I sought to explain true conversion which would expose false conversion through sacraments and rituals. In this fourth book, I am seeking once again to explain true conversion and expose the false teaching that conversion can occur through sacraments, ceremonies, and rituals. A vast majority of churches in the world teach sacramental conversion which leads to massive amounts of false conversions in churches. Many of the ones that I love refuse to be humbled and repent from teaching this. The list of churches that teach such sacramental conversion include:

- Eastern Orthodox Church
- Oriental Orthodox Church
- Greek Orthodox Church
- Assyrian Orthodox Church
- Lutheran Church
- Anglican Church denominations
- United Methodist Churches
- United Church of Christ
- Many more churches

Lastly, this book is written for the glory of God. The Lord is kind, compassionate, merciful, loving and can save an adulterous, sexually immoral, greedy, and selfish sinner such as me. He is able and desires to save the worst of sinners, of whom I could be considered foremost. To Him who is the King of the ages, immortal, invisible, the only God, be honor and glory forever and ever. Amen.

Acknowledgments

To Laura, Pax, and Keryx. I love you all very much. Be steadfast, immovable, always abounding in the work of the Lord. Love the Lord your God with all your heart, and with all your soul, and with all your mind, and with all your strength. Stand firm in the faith and let nothing move you. Always give yourself fully to the work of the Lord, because you know that your labor in the Lord is not in vain. Be strong in the Lord and His Word. Whatever you do, whether you eat or drink, do it all for the glory of the Lord. Lastly, repent and put your faith in the Lord Jesus Christ. Deny yourself, take up your cross, and follow after Him.

Pastor John Macarthur and Pastor Steve Lawson—Thank you for being faithful pastors, able to handle the Word of Truth. Our family continues to be built up in the faith by your ministries.

Dedication and Prayer

Dedicated to Laura, Pax, and Keryx. Trust and follow the Lord Jesus Christ no matter the cost.

James 4:7–10—*Submit yourselves therefore to God. Resist the devil, and he will flee from you. Draw near to God, and he will draw near to you. Cleanse your hands, you sinners, and purify your hearts, you double-minded. Be wretched and mourn, and weep. Let your laughter be turned to mourning and your joy to gloom. Humble yourselves before the Lord, and he will exalt you.*

Prayer
"Father, have mercy on the blind and hard-hearted in sacramental churches. Open their eyes that they may see the truth of Your gospel, repent, and be saved. Do this all for Your glory. Amen."

Introduction

In this introduction it is my intent to simply state historical truths of this book and lead into the text of interest, James 4:7–10. This book has historically been credited to James, the half-brother of Christ (Mark 6:3). It is estimated that the letter was written around AD 44–49 and was written to believers who had been scattered because of persecution. Many commentators and theologians highlight how James was influenced by the Lord's teaching as he makes several statements that can be traced back to the Sermon on the Mount as well as many more of the Lord's teachings.

Theologians have suggested several ways to outline this book. Some have suggested that it should be viewed as a book on living faith. Other theologians would outline this book as a series of tests to examine if one possesses saving faith. Both suggestions would be appropriate. James presents a character of living faith as opposed to a dead faith and the character of saving faith as opposed to a non-saving faith. They are both attributes of saving faith as well as tests of living faith. Below is a helpful outline of the epistle:

- 1:1–12—God tests faith through perseverance in suffering
- 1:13–18—God tests faith through the temptation of blaming
- 1:19–27—God tests faith by response to the Word

- 2:1–13—God tests faith through impartial love
- 2:14–26—God tests faith by righteous works
- 3:1–12—God tests faith through the tongue
- 3:13–18—God tests faith through humble wisdom
- 4:1–6—God tests faith through worldly indulgence
- 4:7–10—**<u>James issues a gospel call to saving faith</u>**
- 4:13–17—God tests faith through dependence
- 5:1–11—God tests faith through patient endurance
- 5:12—God tests faith through truthfulness
- 5:13–18—God tests faith through prayerfulness
- 5:19–20—God tests faith through evangelistic love

It is important to note that the book of James in no way clashes with the doctrine of justification by faith in Christ. James notes that saving faith is in the Lord Jesus Christ (James 2:1) and he also cites Genesis 15:6 just as Paul does in Romans 4:3 when Paul is explaining that one is forensically declared righteous through faith in Christ. Therefore, both James and Paul agree that *faith in Christ* is the means to receiving righteousness and that *works* are the verification of saving faith. There are certainly more thorough books that have been written that can cover the specifics on James such as information on the author, date, background and setting, historical and theological themes, and interpretive challenges, but this very brief intro will suffice for the purposes of this book.

The boldfaced section of James 4:7–10 is where we will start chapter 1. However, it is helpful to get a running start as we enter chapter 1 of this book. We'll start in James 4:1 which will help us segue into James 4:7.

James 4:1—*What causes quarrels and what causes fights among you? Is it not this, that your passions are at war within you?*

James is noting that there is fighting within the church. Just as Jesus promised there would be wheat among the tares, so James is warning against such quarrels. In fact, James comments that there are *polemos* from which we get *polemics*. *Polemos* means "war," "battle," "strife," or "warfare." He also comments that there is *maché* which is "contention," "quarrel," or "combat." He also notes that there is *hédoné* which is where we get hedonism. *Hédoné* means "pleasure" or "sensual pleasure" and alludes to what is enjoyable to the natural senses. This word has a negative connotation that speaks of the satiation of bodily desires and lusts. Essentially, James is noting that there are professing believers who are at war with one another, who are in contention with one another, and who are giving way to sensual pleasure.

James 4:2–3—*You desire and do not have, so you murder. You covet and cannot obtain, so you fight and quarrel. You do not have because you do not ask. You ask and do not receive, because you ask wrongly, to spend it on your passions*

Here, there are five more characteristics that mark these people as unbelievers in the Church; they are murderous, coveting, fighting, quarreling, and not asking God in faith. This vice list is shorter, but it is reminiscent of Jesus giving His disciples a list of sins on how a person is defiled in Matthew 15:19, "For out of the heart come evil thoughts, murder, adultery, sexual immorality, theft, false witness, slander." The professing church members were marked by worldly behavior which gave evidence of an unconverted and unregenerate life.

James 4:4—*You adulterous people! Do you not know that friendship with the world is enmity with God? Therefore whoever wishes to be a friend of the world makes himself an enemy of God*

James has gotten right down to the bottom line of what it means to be unrepentantly murderous, covetous, quarrelsome, combative, and hedonistic. Such behavior is evidence of being unregenerate. James says it another way when he calls them *"adulterous."* The use of this word is very familiar Old Testament language where the prophets used such language to describe Israel and Judah being unfaithful to the LORD. In Jeremiah 3:6–10, Israel is confronted with spiritual adultery where it says, "The Lord said to me in the days of King Josiah: 'Have you seen what she did, that faithless one, Israel, how she went up on every high hill and under every green tree, and there played the whore? And I thought, "After she has done all this she will return to me," but she did not return, and her treacherous sister Judah saw it. She saw that for all the adulteries of that faithless one, Israel, I had sent her away with a decree of divorce. Yet her treacherous sister Judah did not fear, but she too went and played the whore. Because she took her whoredom lightly, she polluted the land, committing adultery with stone and tree. Yet for all this her treacherous sister Judah did not return to me with her whole heart, but in pretense, declares the Lord.'"

James is charging those who are marked by sinful and unrepentant behavior as those who are actually committing spiritual adultery against the Lord. Such a person who would try to be friends of the world and also friends with God is actually an enemy of God. Such a person who tries to put one foot in the world and have one foot in with God is at war with God and is an enemy of God. Jesus would echo James' comment where Jesus said this in Matthew 6:24, "No one can serve two masters, for either he will hate the one and love the other, or he will be devoted to the one and despise the other. You cannot serve God and money." James would fully agree with the Lord that you cannot have two primary loves. You cannot love the world and God. You cannot love money and God. You cannot love yourself and God for you will ultimately choose one over the other. Such a person that tries to be friends with the world and with God is actually a spiritual adulterer.

James 4:5—*Do ye think that the Scripture saith in vain, the spirit that dwelleth in us lusteth to envy?*

In this section, I have used the King James translation as I believe it captures best what James is trying to say. There are different translations of this verse, however, this version captures exactly what James is saying. James is essentially saying that the Scriptures are declaring that man's inner spirit is inclined and lusts to sin and evil. He is stating a biblical truth that man's natural state is one of wickedness and sin. We could very easily survey the Old Testament to see what James is saying about man's sinful depravity. In Jeremiah 13:23, it says this of man's sinful and persistent state, "Can the Ethiopian change his skin or the leopard his spots? Neither can you do good who are accustomed to doing evil." Psalm 7:14 says this of man's perpetual wickedness, "Behold, the wicked man conceives evil and is pregnant with mischief and gives birth to lies." Ecclesiastes 7:20 says of man's sinful depravity, "Surely there is not a righteous man on earth who does good and never sins." In Psalm 51:5, David says this of his corrupted nature due to sin, "Behold, I was brought forth in iniquity, and in sin did my mother conceive me." Additionally, in Genesis 6:5, it says this regarding man's proclivity and ability to sin and inability to do good, "The LORD saw that the wickedness of man was great in the earth, and that every intention of the thoughts of his heart was only evil continually." Simply put, James is saying that Scripture does not talk about man's lust to envy in vain. In fact, Scripture is quite clear that man is so corrupt in his whole nature and being that he continually lusts to envy and sin. James is saying that those who are acting out this natural sinful proclivity with no repentance are those that are unregenerate and unconverted.

James 4:6—*But he gives more grace. Therefore it says, "God opposes the proud but gives grace to the humble."*

This is where we'll transition into chapter 1. For those that are worldly, unconverted, and unregenerate, God does not leave people in such a helpless estate. God is merciful, kind, and compassionate, and where sin abounds, grace abounds more. James is saying that though there are those who have friendship with the world, are enemies with God, are committing spiritual adultery against the Lord, and are in warfare with God, that God will give grace to the humble. James will transition into a gospel call in verses 7–10 that contain ten verbs in the aorist tense and imperative mood which represent a call to saving faith. These are:

- Submit—*hupotassó*
- Resist—*anthistémi*
- Draw near—*eggizó*
- Cleanse—*katharizó*
- Purify—*hagnizó*
- Grieve—*talaipóreó*
- Mourn—*pentheó*
- Weep—*klaió*
- Turn—*metastrephó*
- Humble—*tapeinoó*

We'll take a look at each one of these commands and see how they are a gospel call to saving faith, attributes of saving faith, as well as James' deep understanding and theology of conversion which was clearly influenced by the Lord Jesus Christ. Even more amazing is that the tenth command to humble oneself before the Lord is a summation of the previous nine verbal commands that sum up a humble person who receives God's saving grace. Let's get started.

CHAPTER 1

The Gospel Call for Submissive and Obedient Faith toward the Lord Jesus Christ

James 4:7—*<u>Submit therefore to God</u>. But resist the devil, and he will flee from you.*

The first aorist imperative and characteristic of saving faith that James gives is to submit to God. The word *submit* comes from *hupotassó* which means "to place or rank under" or "to subject." It is a compound word that comes from *hypo* which means "under" and *tássō* which means "arrange." Properly, it means "to be under God's arrangement or submitting to the Lord and His plan."

Hupotassó is a military term which means "to draw up in order of battle to form, array, and marshal soldiers and military vessels." This word meant that soldier divisions were to be arranged in a fashion under the command of the leader. The soldier divisions were in subjection to the orders of their commander and were, thus, ready to carry out warfare. Not only was this word used in a military setting, but it was also used when describing subjection in relationships or in civilian life. This word can also carry with it a quality of submission, meaning that the one submitting is doing so with reverence, self-sacrificially, obediently from the heart, respectfully, willingly, and lovingly.

So, what would James have had in mind when it came to submitting to God? Did James think this submission to God was simply a confession of a creed and answering some questions about the Christian faith? Did James think this submission to God was to rotely and mechanically read a confession and absolution and have a pastor forgive you all your sins? Or rather, did the half-brother of Jesus see and hear the Lord's gospel invitation to submit oneself, trust the Lord, and follow Him? When talking about reverent submission, James would have surely been aware of Christ's gospel invitations where Christ called for a submissive and obedient trust in Him. We will exposit the Lord's gospel invitation found in Matthew, Mark, and Luke's written accounts where the Lord called for a submissive, meek, and obedient faith (Matthew 16:24–26, Mark 8:34–37, Luke 9:23–26). Let's see how James' call to submit to God would have been influenced by the gospel invitation of the Lord Jesus Christ.

Christ's Call for a Submissive, Meek Faith

Matthew 16:24—*Then Jesus said to his disciples, "If anyone wants to come after me, he must deny himself, take up his cross, and follow me.*

Mark 8:34—*And he summoned the crowd together with His disciples, and said to them, "If anyone wants to come after me, he must deny himself, take up his cross, and follow me.*

Luke 9:23—*And he was saying to them all, "If anyone wants to come after me, he must deny himself, take up his cross daily, and follow me."*

Jesus never hid His cost of what it meant to be one of His disciples or what it meant to be a believer in Him. The crowd that had gathered with Jesus were made up of true disciples who had left everything to follow Him (Matthew 4:19). There was one of Jesus' twelve disciples that followed Him but was unregenerate and unconverted, Judas (John 6:70). There were people in the crowd who were amazed at His teaching but were uncommitted (Luke 4:32). There were people that followed Him because of His miracles but were uncommitted (John 6:2) There were people that followed Him because He provided food for them but were uncommitted (John 6:26–27). Jesus' own brothers may have followed Him, but did not believe in Him, including James (John 7:5). The crowd that followed Jesus was mixed with the committed, the curious, and the counterfeit. The crowd that followed Jesus was mixed with the faithful, the feigned, and the false. The crowd that followed Jesus was mixed with the sincere, the skeptical, and the pseudo.

The crowd and religious leaders were faced with making a decision on Jesus based on His claims of Himself and the works He was doing (John 5:36). However, there were always obstacles that came along with following Jesus. Jesus' teaching caused many of His disciples to depart from Him (John 6:66). Jesus' message to religious Jews that they were poor, blind, prisoners, and oppressed caused them to want to kill Him (Luke 4:19–29). Jesus' healing on the Sabbath caused the religious leaders to want to kill Him (Mark 3:6). Jesus' claim to deity caused people and religious leaders to stumble (Luke 5:21–25). Jesus' claim to be one with God the Father caused the Jewish leaders to want to kill Him (John 5:16–18). Jesus casting out demons into pigs caused great fear in an entire city and they asked Him to leave (Luke 8:37). There was always a decision to be made on how to respond to the person and work of the Lord Jesus Christ.

First, notice that Christ's invitation to follow Him is for everyone. Christ's call to follow Him in a salvific way was and is open to everyone. Christ would turn to both His disciples and to the crowd when He issued the call. Jesus didn't hide this invitation in the fine print. Jesus didn't whisper this call. Jesus didn't issue this call to only a select few. No, Jesus Christ invited all people everywhere to follow Him. To the committed followers, this was a reminder of the call they answered and an exhortation to follow Him with deep commitment. For those that were unconvinced, undecided, and opposed, this served as a clarion call to come to and follow Christ in a salvific way. This invitation rang out to the crowds 2,000 years ago and the invitation remains open to all people everywhere today.

Second, notice that the one who issues the call also defines the terms of how He will be followed. Mankind can only follow Jesus Christ on His terms. There are no escape clauses. There is no bargaining with the terms. There is no negotiating with the terms. Jesus is the one who defines the terms on what it means to be His disciple, to be a believer, to be His slave. Jesus is the one who defines how to enter the Narrow Gate (Matthew 7:13–14). Jesus is the one who defines how to enter the kingdom of God (Mark 1:15). Jesus is the one who defines how to enter the kingdom of heaven (Matthew 4:17). This is the call that the Lord Jesus Christ has put forth. You will either accept this call or deny this call. You can embrace the call or ignore the call, but how you respond to this call determines all eternity for you. How you respond to this call determines whether you lose your soul or keep your soul.

Third, notice that Jesus knew that all types of people would desire to come to Him in a salvific way. The word *wants* comes from *theló* which means to "wish," "desire," "intend," or "to be willing." *Theló* carries with it the desire, wish, or intention to follow a course of action. Jesus knew that the religious Jew, the down-and-out prostitute, the despised tax collector, the desperate leper, the half-breed Samaritan, the detested Gentile, the desolate paralytic, the religious teacher, the religious leader, and others would desire to receive salvation from Him. Likewise, even today, Jesus knows that the religious Catholic bishop, the religious Lutheran, the religious Eastern Orthodox churchgoer, the opioid addict, the porn addict, the self-righteous professing Christian, the practicing homosexual, the crooked businessman, the moral but lost grandparent, and many other people would be desiring salvation through Him. Jesus wasn't looking for a large number of disciples. Jesus was looking for the quality of the disciple. For all those desiring to come after Him in a salvific way, Jesus wanted everyone to be crystal clear on what it meant to be a believer, a disciple, and a follower of Him. Jesus didn't want people to be self-deceived. Jesus didn't want people to be misguided followers of Him. Therefore, for all people who would seek to be followers of His and even those that would reject, He issued this call.

Fourth, notice that the first command He gives to the crowd is to *"deny himself"* which is given in the aorist tense and imperative mood. The word *deny* comes from the original word *aparneomai*. *Aparneomai* is a compound word with *apó* mean "from" and *arnéomai* meaning "deny." The prefix *apó* intensifies *arnéomai* and the word *aparneomai* means to "deny," "disown," "repudiate," or "disregard." Properly, *aparneomai* means "to strongly deny." It means "to utterly deny that which was originally refused." It is important to note that this verb is in *aorist tense and imperative mood* which simply means that it is "a command that signifies and calls for a one-time activity or the completion of an activity." Unlike a *verb,* which is a *present imperative,* meaning the action is commanded to be followed in the present tense, the *aorist imperative* calls for the completion of the action. Therefore, we can know that Jesus is calling for a decisive self-denial for anyone that would desire to be His disciple.

Jesus used this word, *aparnéomai,* when prophesying Peter's denial of Him. Peter's first denial of Jesus was in front of a servant girl who said to Peter in Matthew 26:69, "You too were with Jesus the Galilean," and Peter responded to her in Matthew 26:70, "I do not know what you are talking about." Peter's second denial took place with another slave woman who saw Peter and said to him in Matthew 26:71, "This man was with Jesus of Nazareth," and Peter took an oath and responded in Matthew 26:72 by saying, "I do not know the man." Peter's third denial came when he was approached by some where they said in Matthew 26:73, "You really are one of them as well, since even the way you talk gives you away," and Peter cursed and swore and said to them in Matthew 26:74, "I do not know the man!"

So, what does it mean when Jesus called for self-denial? In Jesus' ministry, He was very clear on what was included with self-denial. Jesus would call for a denial of self-righteousness (Luke 18:9–14). Jesus called for a self-denial of works-righteousness salvation (Matthew 5:20). Jesus called for a self-denial of the love of money (Matthew 6:24). Jesus called for a self-denial of false religion (Matthew 15:12–14). Jesus called for a self-denial of following the world and the deceitfulness of wealth (Matthew 13:22). Jesus called for a denial of loving the world (John 15:19). Jesus called for the self-denial of living for worldly comfort (Luke 9:57–58). Jesus called for the self-denial of other relationships taking preeminence over Him (Luke 14:26, Matthew 10:34–38). Jesus called for a self-denial of running one's own life (Luke 14:26). Jesus called for a self-denial and repentance of one's sin. Jesus' call to deny oneself is a radical call of repentance, submission, and faith in Him. Just as Peter said, "I do not know the man," so all true believers in Christ are called to say the same thing to our sinful, self-righteous, self-willed, and self-absorbed way of life. This is a call to be done living for yourself. It was a call to stop being the lord of your life. Jesus is calling you to deny the unholy trinity of me, myself, and I. This is a call to repent of your sins, say goodbye to your worldly desires and pride, say goodbye to self-will, self-sufficiency, self-wishes, and self-righteousness in exchange for the Lord Jesus Christ's yoke, His will, and His rule over your life. Jesus called for a submission unto Him by saying goodbye to one's life.

Let's also note that it is a self-denial that encompasses the whole of one's person which includes one's mind, one's heart, one's will, one's soul, and one's body. There is not one single element of one's person that is not included in "deny himself" or "deny yourself." In Hebrew, the heart is the center of one's being. It is not merely the home of one's affections, but also the seat of the will and moral purpose. The condition of one's heart determined one's influence. In Proverbs 4:23, it says this regarding the heart, "Watch over your heart with all diligence, for from it flow the springs of life." Jesus warned that true defilement came from the heart in Matthew 15:18–19, where He said, "But the things that come out of the mouth come from the heart, and those things defile the person. For out of the heart come evil thoughts, murders, acts of adultery, other immoral sexual acts, thefts, false testimonies, and slanderous statements." The denying of oneself was to deny the whole of oneself. In fact, Jesus clarifies this in Matthew 16:25–26, where He says, "For whoever wants to save his **life** will lose it; but whoever loses his **life** for my sake will find it. For what good will it do a person if he gains the whole world, but forfeits his **soul**? Or what will a person give in exchange for his **soul**?" The words *life* and *soul* come from the original word *psuché*. *Psuché* can mean "the human soul," "the soul as the seat of affections and will," "the self," "a human person," "an individual," or a "life." It is a person's distinct identity. Kenneth S. Wuest says this of *psuché* which is, "that part of man which wills, and thinks, and feels, or in other words, to the will power, the reason, and the emotions, to the personality with all his activities, hopes and aspirations." Jesus was calling for the whole of one's body and soul to be submitted to Him. No longer would one's personal knowledge and wisdom be the driving force, but rather, it would be substituted for the knowledge and wisdom of the Lord Jesus Christ. Christ is not calling for sinless perfection. May it never be! What Christ is calling for is the renunciation, denunciation, and repudiation of one's life. Jesus is calling for commitment, submission, devotion, dedication, faithfulness, fidelity, and loyalty of one's life unto Him. It is a self-denial that will not learn, think, and act apart from God's Word but will learn, think, and act on sin, salvation, the Bible, theology, the church, living, marriage, money, family, job, eternity, and everything else according to God's Word. William Macdonald says this on self-denial, "There are 'No-No's' in that school which we must learn to renounce." In other words, the self-denying Christian must learn to say "yes" and not "no" to Jesus' commands.

Fifth, notice that there is a second command which is to *"take up a cross."* The word *take up* is also written in the *aorist imperative*, simply meaning that it is "a command that signifies and calls for a one-time activity or the completion of an activity." This is a command to make a final decision to not only deny yourself, but to also die to yourself. Notice that this is not cross-wearing, it is cross-bearing. Bearing a cross 2,000 years ago had a very specific meaning. *Bearing a cross* meant strapping an instrument of death on your back. It was a walk of death that included disgrace, shame, pain, and persecution. Disgrace was guaranteed. Shame was promised. Pain was a certainty. Persecution was inevitable. Jesus was calling for a self-denying, cross-bearing, Christ-identifying walk where a person would so identify with Him that they would do so even to the point of death. Notice in Luke's account that Christ says this cross-bearing would be daily. A cross-bearing death to self was to be the walk and manner of one's life. Cross-bearing was not glorious. In fact, the Jews would have been very familiar with this picture as the Proconsul Varus crucified 2,000 Jews who besieged Sabinus and made an example of them and their insurrection.

Crucifixion to the point of death on the cross could take from six hours to several days and could be due to the aftereffects of compulsory scourging, maiming, hemorrhage, and dehydration causing hypovolemic shock. Death could also be precipitated by cardiac arrest. The Roman guards would not leave the site until the victim was dead. They could kill the victim by breaking the victim's legs, stabbing the heart or chest with spears, or building a fire at the foot of the cross to asphyxiate the victim. This statement by Jesus would have been shocking. As we noted earlier, just as one was to deny the unholy trinity of me, myself, and I, they were also called to repent and die to worldly desires, die to pride, die to self-will, die to self-sufficiency, die to self-wishes, and die to self-righteousness. They were to live for Christ's yoke, Christ's will, and Christ's rule over their life. This is a step of self-humiliation. This is a step of self-renunciation. Taking up one's cross is to die to self and surrender and submit to the King of heaven, the Lord Jesus Christ.

Sixth, notice Jesus' third command which is to *"follow me."* The word *follow* comes from *akoloutheó* which means "to follow the one who precedes," "to join one as an attendant," or "to accompany one." Properly, this means "to be in the same way with." It carries the idea of cleaving steadfastly to one and to conform wholly to that one's example in living and, if need be, in dying also. It is a strong word that gives the idea that the one following is not following begrudgingly but is willfully following step for step with Christ. The one following isn't resentfully following, but rather, is seeking to follow Christ wholeheartedly. The self-denying, cross-bearing follower is conforming their mind to that of Christ to mimic Christ in thought, word, deed, and intent. Let's also notice that unlike the previous two commands which were in the aorist imperative, this command is in the present imperative. The *present imperative* signifies that it is a command that is to be continually followed. Jesus is defining the call to submissive saving faith. It is to make the conclusive decision to deny yourself, die to yourself, and to follow Christ wherever He goes as a self-denying, cross-bearing follower. You cannot follow Christ without denying yourself. You cannot follow Christ without taking up your own cross. You cannot change Christ's terms. You cannot wipe away these verses. You cannot bargain with the

Way, the Truth, and the Life (John 14:6). Heaven and earth will pass away, but Christ's Word will not pass away (Matthew 5:18, 1 Peter 1:24–25).

Jesus gave several examples where following Him was connected with hearing and doing. Jesus was very clear on the importance of submissive listening and following. Jesus explained that His sheep would be those that listened and followed Him where He says this in John 10:3–4, "To him the gate keeper opens. The sheep **hear** his voice, and he calls his own sheep by name and leads them out. When he was brought out all his own, he goes before them, and the sheep **follow** him, for they know his voice." Likewise, Jesus made a similar statement about a grain of wheat needing to die before it bore fruit, that one must lose one's life to save it, and that His servants would be faithful followers of Him where He says this in John 12:24–26, "Truly, truly, I say to you, unless a grain of wheat falls into the earth and dies, it remains alone; but if it dies, it bears much fruit. Whoever loves his life loses it, and whoever hates his life in this world will keep it for eternal life. If anyone serves me, he must **follow** me; and where I am, there my servant will be also; if anyone serves me, the Father will honor him." Jesus would go on to say that those who hear His words and does them is a wise man whereas those who hear His Word and don't act upon them are foolish (Matthew 7:24–27). Jesus would pronounce that those who hear His Word and keep it are those who are blessed where He says this in Luke 11:28, "Blessed rather are those who **hear** the word of God and **keep it**!" When Jesus was calling all people to follow Him in a salvific way, it was a call to submissive, self-denying, cross-bearing, obedient faith. When Jesus stops, His sheep would stop. When Jesus would turn left, His sheep would turn left. Jesus' sheep would learn to think of prayer according to Jesus (Matthew 6:5–15, Luke 18:1–18). Jesus' sheep would learn to think of sin according to Jesus (Matthew 5:21–22, 27–30). Jesus' sheep would learn how to think about His teaching (John 8:31). Jesus' sheep would learn how to live in a fallen world (Matthew 5:13–16). Jesus' sheep would learn how to think of Him (Matthew 12:8, 16:16; Luke 24:46–47; John 6:35, 48, 51; 8:12, 58; 9:5; 10:7, 9, 11, 14; 11:25; 15:1). Jesus' sheep would learn to think of marriage according to Him (Matthew 19:1–10). Jesus' sheep would learn to think of handling persecution according to Him (Matthew 10:16–25). Jesus' sheep would learn how to forgive according to Him (Matthew 18:21–35). This is all to say that Jesus was calling for a self-denying, submissive faith in Him that would willingly follow Him wherever He went.

Another way to describe a self-denying, cross-bearing follower of Christ can be understood through how the writers of the New Testament identified themselves. Many of the New Testament writers identified themselves as a *doulos* or slave. The title of being a slave has negative connotations now, but that title doesn't bear that stigma when it comes to being a slave of Christ in the New Testament. A *doulos* in the New Testament and, as used by Peter and Paul, was one who willingly committed himself to serve a master he loves and respects. The *doulos* had no life of his own, no will of his own, no purpose of his own, and no plan of his own. All things were subject to his master. Every thought, breath, and effort were subject to the will of his master. The *doulos* was one who was absolutely surrendered and totally devoted to his master. The existence of the *doulos* was for the will and purpose of his master and nothing else.

Paul referred to himself as a slave or *doulos* of Christ (Romans 1:1, Philippians 1:1, Titus 1:1). Paul referred to Timothy as a *doulos* of Christ (Philippians 1:1). James referred to himself as a *doulos* of Christ even though he was half-brother to Jesus (James 1:1). Peter referred to himself as a *doulos* of Christ (2 Peter 2:1). Jude referred to himself as a *doulos* of Christ even though he was half-brother to Jesus (Jude 1:1). John referred to himself as a *doulos* of Christ (Revelation 1:1). Jesus referred to a true believer that did His will as His faithful *doulos* (Matthew 25:21). Jesus said that those who were a true *doulos* of His would do the things He commanded (Luke 17:10). Jesus told the Jewish leaders that there was a *doulos* to sin, but if the Son sets one free, they would be free indeed, or rather, a child of God (John 8:34–42).

Conversely, the one who claimed allegiance to Christ but never did His work was a wicked and lazy *doulos* (Matthew 25:26). The one who claimed allegiance to Christ but never denied self, bore a cross, and followed Him was self-deceived and Jesus says this of them in Matthew 7:21–23, "Not everyone who says to me, 'Lord, Lord' will enter the kingdom of heaven, but the one who does the will of my Father who is in heaven will enter. Many will say to me on that day, 'Lord, Lord, did we not prophesy in your name, and in your name cast out demons, and in your name perform many miracles?' And then I will declare to them, 'I never knew you; leave me, you who practice lawlessness.'" Even though many people would and will do works in Christ's name, He claims that they were never saved, regenerated, or converted into His kingdom. The word "never" comes from *oudepote* with *oude* meaning "not" and *pote* meaning "at one time or other." Essentially, when Jesus says, "I never knew you", He is saying that there was never a point in time that He ever savingly knew those who claimed allegiance to Him.

Please note that the true believer has no rights. The true believer has no vote. Jesus becomes the exclusive Lord of the believer's life. Jesus is not following the believer. Jesus is not the copilot of the true believer's life. Jesus is not sitting in the back seat and following where you go. No, at salvation, the believer denies self, dies to self, and takes the leap of saving faith to follow Christ. The believer does not know where the Lord will lead, but the believer will obediently and submissively follow the Lord regardless of where He leads them. The world, the flesh, family, friends, and one's own understanding are not being followed. The Lord Jesus Christ is the one being followed. Charles Spurgeon has said this of this call to salvation, "There are no crown-wearers in heaven that were not cross-bearers here below."

Matthew 16:25—*For whoever wants to save his life will lose it; but whoever loses his life for my sake will find it.*
Mark 8:35—*For whoever wants to save his life will lose it, but whoever loses his life for my sake and the gospel's will save it.*
Luke 9:24—*For whoever wants to save his life will lose it, but whoever loses his life for my sake, this is the one who will save it.*

Jesus will now give his listeners the ultimate paradox. The paradox is that if you would hold on to your life, you will lose it. If you hold on to your priorities, hold on to your own purpose, hold on to your personal agenda, hold on to false religion, and continue to be lord of your life, then you will lose your life eternally. However, if you will lose your life for the sake of the Lord Jesus Christ and the gospel, you will save it. This is the paradox. You must lose your life to gain it. You must die to live. It is important to notice that the word *life* is translated from *psuché* which can also be translated as the "soul." As we learned earlier, the soul is the home of one's affections and the seat of the will and moral purpose. Is the Lord Jesus Christ worth denying yourself, dying to yourself, and following Him or is there more worth in remaining the lord over your life? There must be a crucifixion before there is a resurrection. You cannot serve two masters as you will ultimately love one and hate the other (Matthew 6:24). You are either with Jesus or you are against Him (Luke 11:23). You either gather with Jesus or you scatter (Matthew 12:30). There are no fence straddlers. There are only those for Christ and those opposed to Christ.

Notice that the one who loses his life, or rather soul, for Christ's sake and the gospel will save it. Whoever denies the self, takes up their cross, and decides to follow the biblical Jesus will find their life, or rather, eternal life. Eternal life is not just speaking of the quantity of life, meaning eternality. It is also speaking of a new quality of life. The word *eternal* comes from *aiónios* and means "age-long" or "unending." *Aiónios* certainly has in mind the quantity of time, but it also carries with it the quality of a particular age. It can mean the unique reality of God's life in the soul of a man or God's life at work in the believer. Thus, believers who have eternal life are those who experience the quality of God's life now as a present possession. To have eternal life is to have a brand-new quality of life. This means that the believer will have abundant life (John 10:10). This means they will have new life (John 3:3). This means they will have a new quality of life (John 3:16). This means that Christians will now be swimming upstream rather than floating downstream with the world and false religion. As James would say, friendship with the world is enmity with God (James 4:4). The Christian will have lost their life to gain it. What once was up is now down. The world's way is now seen as the wrong way and Christ's way is the only way. This is the paradox of losing your life to find it in Christ and the foolishness of holding on to one's life, but ultimately losing it eternally.

When James gave the command to submit to God, we should see the radical call to submission that Jesus called for and how James would have understood submission unto God. James, who was a prominent leader in the Jerusalem church, would have surely known what it meant to submit to God. James, the half-brother of Jesus, who did not initially believe in the Lord Jesus Christ, would surely understand submission unto God through Christ (John 7:5, 14:6). James understood that a saving faith in the Lord Jesus Christ was a submissive, meek faith (James 4:7).

Matthew 16:26—*For what will it profit a man if he gains the whole world and forfeits his soul? Or what shall a man give in return for his soul?*

Mark 8:36–37—*For what does it profit a man to gain the whole world and forfeit his soul? For what can a man give in return for his soul?*

Luke 9:25—*For what does it profit a man if he gains the whole world and loses or forfeits himself?*

Jesus is calling for everyone to do a spiritual accounting assessment. Since there are two options that will account for one's spiritual destiny, this decision will require the utmost diligence. In other words, do a hypothetical spiritual equation. If you could have all the money in the world, become king over every nation, own all the land, own every possession, and control the whole world system, what good would this be if you lose your soul and go to hell? If you could gain the approval of all mankind but not have the approval of God, what would you have gained? If you could gain everything the world has to offer for a finite period of time, but ultimately lose your soul and go to hell for all eternity which is a place of God's full wrath and is a place of blackest darkness (Jude 13, Matthew 22:13), filled with furious and concentrated fire everywhere (Matthew 13:42), where there is weeping and anger against God for the unrepentant Christ-rejecting and Christ-neglecting sinners (Matthew 8:12), where they will spend all eternity paying for every sin they've ever committed with no hope of escape (Luke 16:26) and only the expectation of excruciating torments to their body, soul, and spirit (Matthew 10:28) and an undying conscience that will haunt them day and night, forever and ever. with no reprieve (Luke 16:25); what have you gained? If you get to be lord of your life for a few years, but lose it forever, what have you profited? The fact of the matter is that you'll never own the whole world. You'll never control the world system. Jesus asks an impossible hypothetical question to his audience. You'll never be king over every nation. You'll never own everything in the world, but even if you could, what have you profited if you eternally forfeit your soul? Only a fool would hang on to creation and forsake the Creator. Only a fool would serve money rather than the Master. Only a fool would serve immorality rather than Immanuel. Only a fool would serve sexual licentiousness rather than the Sovereign Lord. Only a fool would serve a job rather than Jesus. Only a fool would serve the self rather than the Savior. Only a fool would serve a false Christianity rather than follow Christ. Only a fool would serve "me" rather than the Messiah.

Not only is a spiritual accounting necessary, but there is also an assessment that needs to be done on one's own soul. Jesus asks, "What shall a man give in return for his soul?" In other words, what could possibly be more valuable than one's own soul? The obvious answer is that there is absolutely nothing that could be more valuable than one's own soul, nor is there anything on earth that can be given in exchange for one's soul. This is clearly a call to saving faith. Jesus declares that the eternity of one's soul is at stake. What can a man give in exchange for his soul? The answer is nothing. The soul is the most valuable thing that any person has. The life and soul of an individual is what Jesus is calling for. This is one of the clearest calls to saving faith in Christ. There are several ways one could paraphrase these verses:

- If anyone would come to Me and desire salvation, let him deny himself, let him die to himself, and follow Me daily. For what would it profit a man if he kept his life, but lost his soul?
- If anyone would come to Me and desire to enter the kingdom of heaven, let him repudiate himself, let him mortify himself, and follow Me wherever I go. For if you maintain your position as lord of your life, you will lose it, but if you lose your life for My sake and the gospel, you will save your soul.

These verses are some of the clearest verses on Christ's call to a submissive and obedient faith in Him. When James called his listeners to "submit therefore to God," we can vividly see how this call could be understood with cross-referencing Jesus' call to submit one's life and soul to Him and to deny oneself, take up one's cross, and follow Him. Lastly, we should see that this is clearly a gospel call to saving faith as the response of the individual to Jesus determines whether they lose their soul or save their soul. Did James believe that a faith that would not submit, would not listen, and would not follow Christ could possibly save one's soul? James can answer this question for himself in James 1:22–25:

*But **be doers** of the word, and **not hearers only**, deceiving yourselves. For if anyone is a hearer of the word and not a doer, he is like a man who looks intently at his natural face in a mirror. For he looks at himself and goes away and at once forgets what he was like. But the one who looks into the perfect law, the law of liberty, and perseveres, being no hearer who forgets but a doer who acts, he will be blessed in his doing.*

The Call to Take Your Stand and Oppose the Devil

James 4:7—*Submit therefore to God. **But resist the devil, and he will flee from you**.*

In true repentance, an individual turns away from sin and to God through faith in Jesus Christ. In true repentance, when one turns away from sin, they also turn away from self, sin, and Satan. James' command to resist the devil is to transfer one's allegiance to Christ. This transfer of allegiance is from sin to righteousness. It is a transfer from self to the Savior. It is a transfer from Satan's domain to Christ's dominion. To submit to God and resist the devil are the heads and tails of the same coin.

In James 4:7, James gives another aorist imperative. As we learned earlier, the *aorist tense and imperative mood* simply means that "it is a command that signifies and calls for a one-time completion of an activity or the completion of the action." The word *resist* comes from the original word *anthistémi* which means to "set against," "withstand," "resist," or "oppose." Properly, it means "to take a stand against." Figuratively, it means to establish one's position publicly by conspicuously "holding one's ground" (i.e., refusing to be moved or "pushed back"). This was a military term in Classical Greek meaning "to strongly resist an opponent" or "take a firm stand against." It is a strong word, and it is a term of defense, not offense. To oppose the devil is to stand one's ground by standing firm on the Word of God and obeying it (Luke 11:28). Before we look at opposing Satan, it would first be helpful to understand who Satan is and what we are opposing.

In the Bible, Satan is called the devil (Matthew 4:1), Lucifer (Isaiah 14:12), Beelzebul (Matthew 12:24), Belial (2 Corinthians 6:15), the evil one (Matthew 13:19), the tempter (Matthew 4:3), the ruler of this world (John 14:30), the god of this age (2 Corinthians 4:4), the prince of the power of the air (Ephesians 2:2), the accuser of the brethren (Revelations 12:10), the old serpent (Revelation 12:9), the great dragon (Revelation 12:9), the roaring lion (1 Peter 5:8), Apollyon (Revelation 9:11), the father of lies (John 8:44), the antichrist (1 John 4:3), the ruler of the demons (Matthew 9:34), an angel of light (2 Corinthians 11:14), and more. The names that have been given to the devil rightly characterize who he is.

The name *devil* comes from *diabolos* which means "slanderous" or "falsely accusing." Properly, this is "a false accuser who unjustly criticizes to hurt, malign, and sever a relationship." It can also mean "one who makes charges that bring down and destroy." This characteristic is most prominent in how the devil slanders God's Word. He tempted Eve to believe that God's faithfulness, omniscience, kindness, and character could not be trusted (Genesis 3:1–19). The devil speaks slanderously about God's Word and tries to get man to doubt the reality of the divine standard, doubt God, doubt God's character, doubt God's work, doubt God's love, and doubt God's ability. The devil is a twister, corrupter, and perverter of Scripture (2 Peter 3:16, Matthew 4:1–11). The devil speaks slanderously about the truth of God's Word to bring about the destruction of souls.

The name *Satan* comes *Satanas* and this word means "adversary." The devil is also called the *antichrist* which comes from *antichristos* which means "one who puts himself in the place of Christ" or "against Christ." It is used to describe an opponent of Christ. Both *Satan* and *antichrist* are fitting names for the devil as he is the adversary of God. The devil will oppose everything concerning God. The devil opposes God's standard for male and female (Genesis 1:27) by saying that women can be men and men can be women. The devil opposes God's standard for marriage between a man and a woman (Matthew 19:4–6) by saying that women can marry women and men can marry men. The devil opposes God's standard for murder (Matthew 5:21–22) by saying that women have the right over their body to murder unborn children. The devil opposes God's standard for adultery (Matthew 5:27–28) by saying that adultery is only committing a physical act and that pornography is not adultery. The devil opposes God's standard for righteousness (Matthew 5:20, 48) by saying that ceremonies and sacraments can save someone or give God's righteousness and saving grace. The devil opposes God's Word by causing men to misinterpret Scripture (Luke 11:52). The devil is opposed to everything that is righteous.

The devil is also called *the evil one* which comes from *ponéros* which means "evil," "bad," or "wicked." It is derived from *pónos* which means "pain or laborious labor." Properly, it emphasizes the inevitable agonies and misery that always go with evil. It is used to describe not only evil in nature, but what is viciously evil in its influence and what is actively harmful. This denotes someone who is not content in being corrupt themselves, but also seeking to corrupt others and draw them into the same destruction. What is deeply ominous about this title is that this is the title given to the devil in the parable of the Sower where the devil is the evil one who continually snatches away the salvific Word and message from one's heart (Matthew 13:19, Luke 8:11–12). The devil is actively and willfully set on propagating evil by fighting God and His Word to damn men's souls (Matthew 13:19, Luke 8:12).

The devil is also called *Beelzebub* which means "lord of the flies" or "lord of filth." *Baal* was an ancient pagan word for "lord" and *Zebub* or *Zebul* is translated to "flies." The Ekronites worshipped Beelzebub who was the god of flies as noted in 2 Kings 1:16. Additionally, the word *Zebel* could also be used which meant "dung." Essentially, *Beelzebel* means the "lord of the dung." Over the centuries, this title was used to refer to Satan. This would be a very appropriate title for Satan to essentially say that the devil is lord over everything that is filthy, dirty, worthless, and rotten. Additionally, the name *Belial* is a term which refers to the devil as "the utterly worthless one." Beelzebub, Beelzebel, and Belial all capture the very character of the devil which is that he is utterly worthless because he is the lord over everything filthy, dirty, worthless, and rotten, which is opposed to the Lord.

The title *ruler of this world* is the title Jesus gives to the devil in John 14:30. A similar title that Paul would give the devil was the *prince of the power of the air* (Ephesians 2:2) and the *god of this age* (2 Corinthians 4:4). This is to say that the devil is "the ruler of everything unholy and sinful in the world." The apostle John would describe the devil's rulership this way in 1 John 2:16, "For all that is in the world—the desires of the flesh and the desires of the eyes and pride of life—is not from the Father but is from the world." Paul would describe the devil's rulership this way in Ephesians 2:1–2, "And you were dead in the trespasses and sins in which you once walked, following the course of this world, following the prince of the power of the air, the spirit that is now at work in the sons of disobedience." Paul, John, and Jesus would say that Satan's rulership is one where he proudly and wickedly rules over sexual immorality, impurity, sensuality, idolatry, sorcery, enmity, strife, jealously, fits of anger, rivalries, dissensions, divisions, envy, drunkenness, orgies, adultery, homosexuality, stealing, greediness, revelry, evil thoughts, false witness, slander, crude joking, filthiness, foolish talking, and covetousness (Galatians 5:19–21, 1 Corinthians 6:9–10, Matthew 15:19, Ephesians 5:3–5).

Satan loves pornography. Satan loves homosexual marriage. Satan loves the LGBTQ movement. Satan loves gender fluidity. Satan loves witchcraft. Satan loves murder in the name of religion. Satan loves abortion. Satan loves every kind of theft. Satan loves vandalism. Satan loves materialism. Satan loves dirty jokes. Satan loves when men treat football as more important than church. Satan loves when parents treat their child's sports as more important than the Bible. Satan loves selfishness. Satan loves self-righteousness. Satan loves short tempers. Satan loves corrupt politics. Satan loves the atheist state of North Korea. Satan loves when people follow politics rather than Christ. Satan loves divorce. Satan loves broken homes. Satan loves alcoholism. Satan loves fentanyl addiction. Satan loves smartphone addiction. Satan loves abusive parents. Satan loves rebellious children. Satan loves little white lies. Satan loves every evil thing. Paul gave an admonition in Philippians 4:8 on what the Christian should think about where he says, "Finally, brothers, whatever is true, whatever is honorable, whatever is just, whatever is pure, whatever is lovely, whatever is commendable, if there is any excellence, if there is anything worthy of praise, think about these things." Let us note that Satan hates and opposes all things that are true, honorable, just, pure, lovely, commendable, and excellent.

The devil is also called *an angel of light* by Paul in 2 Corinthians 11:14, where Paul says, "For even Satan disguises himself as an angel of light. So it is no surprise if his servants, also, disguise themselves as servants of righteousness." It is true that Satan is the god of all false religion which includes Hinduism, Buddhism, Taoism, Shintoism, Islam, Judaism, Sikhism, Confucianism, Zoroastrianism, and more. Not only is Satan an angel of light in false religion, he's also an angel of light in false Christianity. Jesus says this about false Christianity in Matthew 24:23–24, "Then if anyone says to you, 'Look, here is the Christ!' or 'There he is!' do not believe it. For false christs and false prophets will arise and perform great signs and wonders, so as to lead astray, if possible, even the elect." Jesus warned that there were going to be false messiahs and false prophets. Likewise, Paul gave a similar statement about false prophets and a false Christianity in 2 Corinthians 11:4, "For if someone comes and proclaims another Jesus than the one we proclaimed, or if you receive a different spirit from the one you received, or if you accept a different gospel from the one you accepted, you put up with it readily enough." Paul warned of false teachers that would proclaim a different Jesus and a different or false gospel.

Satan is the angel of light in Mormonism which teaches Jesus was a spirit child of the heavenly father and heavenly mother. Satan is the angel of light in the Jehovah's Witnesses which teach that Jesus was the archangel Michael before the creation of the world. Satan is the angel of light in the Lutheran, Roman Catholic, Eastern Orthodox, Greek Orthodox, and Anglican churches that teach regeneration, conversion, and salvation through water baptism. Satan is the angel of light in the Unitarian Universal church that teaches that Jesus does not send people to hell. Satan is the angel of light in the Christian Science church which teaches that Mary Baker Eddy's writings are equivalent to the Bible. Satan is the angel of light in Oneness Pentecostalism that denies the Trinity. Satan is the angel of light that teaches purgatory, salvation is by faith plus works, transubstantiation, easy believism with no repentance, anti-Trinitarian doctrine, the prosperity gospel, salvation by ceremonies and sacraments, baptismal regeneration, abhorrent Christology, and more. The *angel of light* title is a proper title of Satan who propagates every abhorrent and heretical form of false religion and false Christianity to oppose Christ and damn men's souls (1 Timothy 4:1–2).

Satan is called the *father of lies* by Jesus in John 8:44. Satan is a master liar. He is a manipulator of the truth. He is skilled in mixing truth with error (Matthew 4:1–11). He is masterful in covering a damning lie with enough truth to make it believable. He is the deceiver of the whole world (Revelation 12:9). He is clever in his falsehood. He is the father of lies and, when he speaks, he speaks out of his own character.

The many names of the devil define his character and works. When James is giving the command to *"resist the devil,"* he is giving a command not only to oppose the devil by submitting to Christ but also standing one's ground against Satan by standing firm on the Word of God by obeying it. *To oppose the devil* is to make a stand against everything he propagates. At salvation, the believer does not know of everything they will be opposing, but it is to say that, at salvation, the believer has come to a place where they have denied themselves, died to themselves, and submitted themselves to Christ, thus, opposing the devil. There is no middle ground. Jesus makes this abundantly clear in Matthew 12:30, where he says, "Whoever is not with me is against me, and whoever does not gather with me scatters." You are either under the rulership of Satan or the lordship of Christ. Becoming a friend of God means becoming an enemy of Satan. At salvation, you take your stance to stand against everything Satan stands for, everything he perpetrates, everything he propagates, everything he instigates. You take your stand against his world system. Previously, you were in bondage to Satan and served him and served yourself. One important point to note is that there are times when a Christian is commanded to flee from things such as sexual immorality (1 Corinthians 6:18), false teachers (John

10:5, 1 Timothy 6:3–11), idolatry (1 Corinthians 10:14), love of money (1 Timothy 6:6–11), and youthful lusts (2 Timothy 2:22). Although James is calling one to stand against the devil and all the devil stands for, there are times when the Christian is commanded to flee the very things the devil propagates.

We should also see that when one comes to saving faith in Jesus Christ and has denied themselves and died to themselves to follow Christ, the devil will flee (James 4:7). In John 14:30, the night of Jesus' betrayal, He said this regarding the devil's power, "I will not speak much more with you, for the ruler of the world is coming, and **he has nothing in me**." Jesus was looking forward to the cross and Jesus saw that the cross meant defeat for Satan. Satan had no claim, power, or authority over Jesus. Paul saw this very same thing where he says in 1 Corinthians 15:56, "The sting of death is sin, and the power of sin is the law." Satan had nothing on Jesus as Jesus was sinless, blameless, and without fault (John 8:46). Jesus' sin-bearing and wrath-taking death on the cross rendered Satan powerless against Him. Paul says it this way in Colossians 2:14–15, "having canceled out the certificate of debt consisting of decrees against us, which was hostile to us; and he has taken it out of the way, having nailed it to the cross. When **he had disarmed the rulers and authorities**, he made a public display of them, **having triumphed over them through him**." At the cross, Satan was a defeated foe. At the moment of salvation for a believer, Satan has no more dominion over the individual. At the moment of salvation, the Holy Spirit indwells a believer (John 7:37–39, Ephesians 1:13, Galatians 3:2, 14). At the moment of salvation, the believer is delivered from the domain of darkness into the kingdom of God's Son (Colossians 1:13). At the moment of salvation, Christ is the one who binds the strong man and plunders the house, or rather, casts out Satan and his demons and indwells the believer and the believer becomes the temple of God (Matthew 12:27–29, 1 Corinthians 6:19). When James is saying that the devil will flee from you, he is stating that the old master leaves because Jesus has purchased redemption for the believer. Satan can still tempt a believer, but he is ultimately vanquished and has no rulership over the believer. This is what James is saying and it is a wonderful promise for every believer.

As we close this chapter, we can see how the aorist imperative commands to "submit therefore to God" and "resist the devil" are the heads and tails of the same coin. Submission of oneself unto God is a self-denying, cross-bearing faith unto God through the Lord Jesus Christ. Likewise, submission unto God is opposition against the devil and everything the devil propagates. Let us keep in mind the submissive and obedient call to faith that James would have had in mind when reflecting on the Lord's gospel invitation. Let's paraphrase James' command as we end this chapter:

"Submit therefore to God by denying yourself, taking up your cross, taking a stand against the devil, and following the Lord Jesus Christ. For what would you profit yourself if you gained the whole world and forfeited your soul? Or what could you give in exchange for your soul?"

CHAPTER 2

The Gospel Call for Preeminent Loving Faith toward the Lord Jesus Christ

James 4:7—*<u>Draw near to God and He will draw near to you</u>. Cleanse your hands, you sinners; and purify your hearts, you double minded.*

The third aorist imperative and characteristic of saving faith that James gives is to draw near to God. The term *draw near* comes from *eggizó* which means "to make near or join one thing to another," "to come near," or "approach." This term expresses "extreme closeness" or "immediate imminence." The term *draw near* is used in the Old Testament regarding the Levitical priestly worship and coming extremely close to God. It is used when the LORD gives instruction to Moses that priests must be consecrated to the LORD when they draw near to Him (Exodus 19:20–22). It is used by the LORD to warn that Aaron and the priests should not draw near to offer the LORD offerings which have defects (Leviticus 21:21). It is used to describe priests coming near to minister to the LORD and offering sacrifices (Ezekiel 43:19, 44:15, 45:4). After the

LORD kills Nadab and Abihu for lighting unauthorized fire, Moses tells Aaron that the LORD will be treated as holy by all those who come near Him (Leviticus 10:1–3). So, we can understand from the Old Testament that *drawing near* carried with it the idea of coming close to the LORD in worship.

In fact, the priests were the ones who would most regularly draw near to the LORD. The priests would wash themselves, offer sacrifices for themselves, and go near the presence of God. On the Day of Atonement, the high priest would go into the Most Holy Place and offer a sacrifice for the nation (Leviticus 16). Therefore, *drawing near* would carry an understanding that the one who drew near to God was one who drew near to Him according to His prescribed instructions for worship.

In the New Testament, *draw near* can be used when referring to the kingdom of heaven drawing near, a time or season drawing near, or drawing near to a location or person. We see *draw near* being used when referring to the kingdom of heaven coming near when John the Baptist is preaching repentance and declaring that the kingdom of heaven is at hand in Matthew 3:2, where he says, "Repent, for the kingdom of heaven is **at hand**." Jesus used *draw near* in a similar way to John the Baptist as Christ was preaching repentance where He says in Matthew 4:17, "Repent, for the kingdom of heaven is **at hand**." We also see *draw near* being used to both show when a time is coming near and a person is coming near as Jesus uses this term to show that the hour of darkness had come and His betrayer had come in Matthew 22:45–46, where He said to His disciples, "Sleep and take your rest later on. See, the hour is **at hand**, and the Son of Man is betrayed into the hands of sinners. Rise, let us be going; see, my betrayer is **at hand**." However, when James is giving a call to "draw near to God," this is not a call to draw near in time or draw near in location. Thus, more explanation is needed on what it means to *draw near*.

We can gain an even greater understanding of what it means to draw near to God by the words of the Lord in an account where the Lord rebuked the Pharisees for their extrabiblical ceremonial washings, neglecting God's commandments, and following man's traditions. In this account, we gain insight on the object that is to draw near to God in Matthew 15:7–9. After the Lord shows that the Pharisees follow the traditions of man rather than the commandments of God, He rebukes them with the following statements:

*"You hypocrites! Well did Isaiah prophesy of you, when he said: 'This people honor me with their lips, but **their heart is far from me**; in vain do they worship me, teaching as doctrines the commandments of men.'"*

Jesus is quoting Isaiah 29:13 and is rebuking the Pharisees for their false worship. Jesus will make a very important statement and declares that the Pharisees' *"heart is far from me."* This a strong indictment that they are false teachers. It is also an indictment of them for offering false worship. The Pharisees were guilty of being both false teachers and offering false worship as their hearts were far from God. Therefore, we can see that a heart that was far away from God was an unsaved, unrepentant, unconverted, unregenerate, and uncircumcised heart (Deuteronomy 10:12–16, 30:6). In the Old Testament, the LORD rebuked Judah for her false worship where they offered sacrifices, prayers, and celebrated festivals, but they were sinful, corrupt, unrepentant, unfaithful, and disobedient (Isaiah 1:2–31). The LORD hated this false worship, and it was a burden to Him (Isaiah 1:14). The LORD spoke again through Amos to Israel on how He despised false religious worship where He rebukes Israel for offering burnt offerings and grain offerings, but worshipping Sikkuth and Kiyyun, which were false gods (Amos 5:21–27). The LORD hated this false worship (Amos 5:21). Again, the LORD was angry with false worship where Israel offered blind, sick, and lame burnt offerings rather than the best animals without defect (Leviticus 1:1–15, Malachi 1:6–14). Therefore, we can see that when Christ indicted the Pharisees with having hearts that were far from God, He had in mind that they were not true worshippers of the LORD and were uncircumcised in heart. A heart that was far from God was an unsaved heart.

The Lord Jesus Christ blasted false worship in the Sermon on the Mount where He corrected a wrong understanding of the attitudes of those who are in the kingdom of heaven (Matthew 5:3–12). The Lord corrected the wrong understanding of righteousness needed to enter the kingdom of heaven (Matthew 5:20). The Lord corrected the wrong understanding of the law as it relates to murder (Matthew 5:21–22) and adultery (Matthew 5:27). The Lord corrected the wrong understanding of false worship in giving (Matthew 6:1–4), praying (Matthew 6:5–14), and fasting (Matthew 6:16–18).

James would know that God wasn't just looking for rote offerings and sacrifices or cold mechanical worship. James would know that God was looking for a heart that would worship Him in spirit and truth (John 4:24). The Lord warned of this throughout His ministry that it was possible to be involved in religious activity but not be saved. It was possible for religious Jews to go to synagogue and be unsaved. The Lord's warnings remain firm today that professing Christians could be religious but have a heart far from God. It is possible for one to pray the Lord's Prayer and have a heart which is far from Christ (Matthew 15:8–9). It is possible to say the Apostle's Creed and Nicene Creed but have a heart which is far from Christ (Luke 6:46–49). It is possible for one to sing Christian songs and have a heart which is far from Christ (Matthew 15:8–9). It is possible for one to give money to a church and have a heart which is far from Christ (Matthew 6:1–4). It is possible for one to be in a Bible-believing church and have a heart which is far from Christ (Matthew 7:21–23). It is possible for one to do work in the church and have a heart which is far from Christ (Matthew 7:21–23). It is possible to be a member in good standing at a church and have a heart which is far from Christ (Matthew 7:21–27). Therefore, **we're able to see that one who is far from the Lord is one who has a heart that is far from the Lord and is thus unsaved, unregenerate, unconverted, and uncircumcised in heart** (Deuteronomy 10:12–16, 30:6).

However, although we know that a heart which is far from God is an unregenerate and uncircumcised heart, we still haven't defined what it means to *draw near to God*. We are able to get an even better understanding of what it means to *draw near to God* when a scribe asked Jesus what the most important commandment is in Mark 12:29–34. Through this interaction, we see what it means when someone draws near to God and enters His kingdom:

And one of the scribes came up and heard them disputing with one another, and seeing that he answered them well, asked him, "Which commandment is the most important of all?" Jesus answered, "The most important is, 'Hear, O Israel: The Lord our God, the Lord is one. ***And you shall** **love** **the Lord your God** **with all your heart** and **with all your soul** and **with all your mind** and **with all your strength**.*' The second is this: 'You shall love your neighbor as yourself.' There is no other commandment greater than these." And the scribe said to him, "You are right, Teacher. You have truly said that he is one, and there is no other besides him. And to love him with all the heart and with all the understanding and with all the strength, and to love one's neighbor as oneself, is much more than all whole burnt offerings and sacrifices." And when Jesus saw that he answered wisely, he said to him,* **"You are not far from the kingdom of God**.*" And after that no one dared to ask him any more questions."*

The scribe asked Jesus a very good question on what the greatest commandment is and Jesus replied that the greatest commandment was to love God with all one's heart, soul, mind, and strength (Matthew 12:37–38). The scribe understood that Jesus gave the right answer (Mark 12:32). The scribe knew that the greatest commandment was not keeping ceremonial or ritualistic external religion, but rather, that keeping the greatest commandment was an internal issue of the heart (Mark 12:32–33). Jesus, acknowledging that the scribe had answered wisely, made a stunning statement to him in Mark 12:34, where He said, "You **are not far** from **the kingdom of God**." When Jesus said the scribe was not far from the kingdom of God, He was telling the scribe that he was unsaved and outside of God's kingdom. The kingdom of God is the "sphere of salvation" or "salvation" and is interchangeable with "the kingdom of heaven." There is a kingdom which means there is a king. Since it is the kingdom of God, God is the King over those who enter His kingdom. The individuals who have inherited eternal life and salvation are those who have entered the kingdom of God. When Jesus told the scribe that he was not far from the kingdom of God, Jesus was telling the man that he was still outside the sphere of salvation. The man was close to the kingdom of God, but he was not in the kingdom of God. Jesus had made many claims to be the Messiah and God and had done many works to substantiate these claims (John 5:36, 10:37–38).

Therefore, Jesus' statement to the scribe indicated that the man was breaking the Shema because he had not lovingly embraced Him as Lord, Christ, and God by faith with all his heart, soul, mind, and strength. The man had correct theology, but he remained condemned and outside the kingdom of God. The man knew the greatest command was to love the Lord with all one's heart, soul, mind, and strength, yet he did not lovingly embrace the Lord Jesus Christ by faith in this way (Mark 12:34). Therefore, we can begin to gain an even better understanding of what it means to *draw near to God*. **To *draw near to God* is to draw near to Him according to His terms and with one's heart by lovingly submitting to the Lord Jesus Christ with all one's heart, soul, mind, and strength by faith and enter an intimate**

relationship with God. This is not to say that when one comes to faith in Christ, they have a perfect faith. However, it is to say that when one comes to faith in Christ, they do so wholeheartedly with loving submission.

So, what would James have in mind when it came to drawing near to God and loving Him with all one's heart, soul, mind, and strength? Was there such a gospel call that was issued by the Lord that called for a preeminent love? Did James recognize that the one drawing near to God was to draw near to God on Christ's terms and not one's own terms? One of the most poignant and clear examples of a gospel invitation that called for one to love Christ with all one's heart, soul, mind, and strength is found in Luke 14:25–33. We will examine Luke 14:25–33 to understand how James' call to draw near to God with one's heart is an echo of Christ's gospel invitation from these verses.

Christ's Call for a Preeminent, Loving Faith

As we approach Luke 14:25–33, we find that Jesus was in His Perean and Judean ministry and Jesus had just finished giving a parable about a great banquet. In the parable of the Great Banquet, a man prepares a banquet and issues an invitation or a *kaleó* which is a summons or an invitation. The man throwing the banquet has his slaves go and issue the invitation (Luke 14:16–17). The preinvited guests were Israel (Luke 14:17). However, the preinvited guests made excuses that they could not attend because they were preoccupied with land (Luke 14:18), possessions (Luke 14:19), and relationships (Luke 14:20). The preinvited guests were not truly interested in the good news of Jesus Christ, salvation, and eternal life. These people demonstrated that they possessed the hearts that were more interested in the cares of the world and the deceitfulness of riches (Matthew 13:23). The man was angry at the preinvited guests and ordered that the slave go and issue the call of the great banquet to everyone else in the city such as the poor, the crippled, the blind, and the lame which would refer to the spiritually destitute in Israel (Matthew 5:3–12, Luke 14:21–22). Finally, the master tells his servant to go into the highways and hedges and compel everyone else to come to his banquet. The people that are invited who are from the highways and hedges are the Gentiles (Luke 14:23). Thus, we see that Jews and Gentiles would be invited to the great banquet. Additionally, the man tells the slave to "compel people to come in." The word *compel* comes from *anagkazó* which means "to compel or constrain while doing so with urgency and a pressing need." It is a strong word and conveys the idea of pressure being applied to bring about an immediate action or decision. This is where we will pick up Luke 14:25–33. Jesus has just given the parable of the Great Banquet and laid out the tragedy of not responding to the invitation to the great banquet. This is where we'll pick up Jesus' gospel invitation for a preeminent loving faith in Him.

Luke 14:25—*Now great crowds accompanied him, and he turned and said to them*

As we noted in the previous chapter, there were many reasons why people would follow Jesus as they were interested in His teaching, miracles, physical provisions, and more. Jesus would now turn to the large crowd and would declare the cost that was required to follow Him. This invitation called for supreme loyalty and love toward the Lord Jesus Christ. It is important to note that Jesus turned to the great crowds when He issued this call. This was a call that needed to be heard by those in the crowd who were the committed, the curious, and the counterfeit. It needed to be heard by those that were the faithful, the feigned, and the false. The call needed to be issued to the sincere, the skeptical, and the pseudo. Those that were true disciples would be reminded of the cost they committed to when they entered the kingdom of God and the commitment which was needed to follow the Lord. Those that were false disciples or uncommitted needed to be reminded of the cost of entry into the kingdom of God. Even today, all faithful servants of Christ are called to issue this call regardless of church membership or church attendance. The size of the crowd is not what was important, what was important was the message and accepting the invitation to follow the Lord Jesus Christ.

Luke 14:26—*"If anyone comes to me and does not hate his own father and mother and wife and children and brothers and sisters, yes and even his own life, he cannot be my disciple."*

First, let's notice that this invitation is open to everyone. As we saw earlier in the parable of the Great Banquet, the invitation goes out to everyone. The invitation is for male and female, Jew and Gentile, barbarian and Scythian, circumcised and uncircumcised, slaves and the free, kings and servants, the wise and the unlearned, the poor and the rich, the religious and the unreligious. The New Testament is a marvelous record of the Lord Jesus Christ saving women (Luke 8:43–48), saving the ceremonially unclean (Luke 5:12–16), saving the paralyzed (Luke 5:17–26), saving despised tax collectors (Luke 5:27–32), saving prostitutes (Matthew 21:31), saving Roman Gentiles (Matthew 8:5–13), saving hardened false teachers such as Paul (Philippians 3:5–9), saving Samaritans (John 4:39–42), saving business owners (Acts 16:11–15), saving physicians (Colossians 4:14), saving pagan worshippers (1 Thessalonians 1:8–10), saving slaves (1 Corinthians 7:21), saving married couples (Acts 18), and more. The invitation is a generous call to all people to come to Christ for salvation.

Second, we should see that Christ is inviting everyone to know who He is which includes His person and His work. When coming to Christ, it is important to know who Jesus is. No one can be saved by a false Jesus. You could put your faith in an anchor but grasping on to an anchor for salvation will drown you, it will not save you. The object of one's faith needs to be the biblical Jesus Christ. Jesus is the Jewish Messiah and Son of the Living God (Matthew 16:16). Jesus is God and He is coequal and coeternal with God the Father and God the Holy Spirit (John 5:17–18; 10:30, 38; 14:10). Jesus is the eternal, Only Begotten, one-of-a-kind, Son of God (John 3:16). Jesus is the Anointed One of God (Luke 4:18–19). Jesus is the Savior of the world (Luke 2:11). Jesus is the Creator and Sustainer of the Universe (John 1:1–14). Jesus is the Son of David (Matthew 1:1–16, Luke 3:23–38). Jesus was born of a virgin (Matthew 1:23). Jesus was the Word made flesh (John 1:14). Jesus was physically born into this world as a man (Matthew 1:25). Jesus is, thus, truly God and truly man.

Not only must we know the person of Jesus, we must also understand His work. Jesus' work is central to the gospel. Jesus lived a sinless life (Matthew 26:59–60) and fulfilled all righteousness found in the law and prophets (Matthew 5:17–20, Luke 24:44–46). He declared Himself to be the Christ (Matthew 16:16), the Only Begotten Son of the Living God through His teaching (John 3:16, Matthew 22:41–46), which was attested to by His miracles and display of divine power (John 10:37–38). Jesus offered Himself as a spotless and blameless sacrifice for sin (John 1:29) to propitiate the righteous anger of God by taking all the sins of God's people (John 10:11) and, thus, the full wrath of God that was due to man (Matthew 26:39, 27:45–46; Luke 22:44). His sacrifice propitiated the righteous anger of God and reconciled and brought peace from man to God and God to man (Matthew 27:51–53, John 19:30). His substitutionary sacrifice and death also redeemed sinful man to Holy God by forgiving man's sin and imputing Christ's righteousness to man (1 Corinthians 5:21, Isaiah 53:1–12). Jesus was resurrected from the dead on the third day by His own power (John 10:18), by God the Father (Galatians 1:1), and by God the Holy Spirit (Romans 8:11), which affirmed

His person, His teachings, and salvific work for sinners (Romans 4:25). He ascended to the right hand of the Father (Luke 24:51) and is empowered with all authority to bring about the plan of salvation for all His people (Matthew 28:18) by causing them to be born again (John 3:1–10) and justified by His grace (John 3:16, 18, 36). He will also return to bring all His own to heaven with Him (John 6:37–40, 14:1–3) to be glorified (John 17:24) while also judging and condemning Satan, demons, and sinful man (Matthew 25:31–46, Revelation 20:7–15). This is the true person and work of Jesus. When coming to Christ for salvation, the person and work of the Lord Jesus Christ should be known and comprehended. Jesus is not calling us to decide without getting to know Him or His work. Just as we would take time to get to know someone before we decide to make a marriage commitment, Jesus invites us to get to know Him. Jesus is inviting us to learn about Him and seek Him through the Scriptures. This is no blind date. This is no quick commitment. Jesus gives the invitation to know His person and work and then commands and demands an answer.

Third, notice that the one issuing the call sets the terms. As we learned earlier in the previous chapter, Jesus is the one who sets the terms for what it means to come to Him for salvation. There is no escape clause. There is no redlining and modifying the terms. There is no negotiating with the one who sets the terms. The terms to come to and follow Jesus in a salvific way are His own terms. As we'll see in this call, there is no redemption without repentance. There is no salvation without submission. There is no salvation without sacrifice. There is no crown without bearing a cross. There is no heaven without holiness. There is no forgiveness without faith. The invitation rings out to everyone, and the call must be answered according to the Lord Jesus Christ's terms. Heaven and earth will pass away, but God's Word will endure forever (Matthew 24:35).

Fourth, we should see that Jesus is calling for one's preeminent faith and love toward Him. Jesus' invitation would most likely be shocking to the crowd who was following Him. The fact that Jesus made a statement of someone hating rather than loving would have most certainly caught the crowd's attention. Although Jesus used the word *hate*, He was not calling for His disciples to turn on those they loved and have an evil disposition toward them. In fact, the Lord explained that we should love our enemies and pray for those who persecute us (Matthew 5:43). The Lord stated that the second greatest commandment was to love your neighbor as yourself (Matthew 22:39). The Lord upheld the fourth commandment when He indicted the Pharisees for cancelling, voiding, and disregarding the fourth commandment to withhold money that could be used to help one's parents (Mark 7:9–13). Therefore, we can see that Christians are called to love and pray for one's enemies, love our neighbor as ourselves, and honor one's parents.

When Jesus was calling for hate, He was showing contrast or preference. The Lord used this same method of showing contrast or preference in Matthew 6:24, where He says, "No one can serve two masters, for either he will hate the one and love the other, or he will be devoted to the one and despise the other. You cannot serve God and money." As in Jesus' example of serving both God and money, Jesus is simply saying that both God and money cannot have the same top priority as you will ultimately love one more than the other. If one loves money, they will hate God. To be devoted to money is to despise God. Matthew 10:37 helps us understand what Christ is saying where He says, "The one who loves father or mother more than me is not worthy of me; and the one who loves son or daughter more than me is not worthy of me." Jesus is purposefully creating extremes. He is pitting the affections of one's most loved ones against their affections to Him. It is important to note that He doesn't start with friends, employers, or acquaintances. No, Jesus starts with those who are in your closest concentric circle. If you are a mother, Jesus is calling for your preeminent love and trust over your children. If you are a daughter, Jesus is calling for your preeminent love and trust over your mother. If you are a happily married husband, Jesus is calling for your preeminent love and trust over your wife. Jesus purposefully starts with the people that mean the most to you. Christ is calling for your preeminent allegiance, love, trust, and affection. Notice that in Matthew 10:37 if one has greater love and affection for anyone other than Him, He states that they are unworthy of Him. The word *worthy* comes from the original word *axios* and means "worthy," "worthy of," or "deserving." Properly, *axios* is the "assessment in keeping with how something weighs in on God's balance scale of truth."

Fifth, we should see that the one who is loving one's father, mother, wife, children, brothers, sisters, or anyone else more than the Lord Jesus Christ cannot be His disciple. The word *disciple* comes from the word *mathétés* which is "a learner, a disciple or a pupil." It was typical in Jewish culture for rabbis to be followed and have students or disciples. The disciples of rabbis would follow the rabbi to learn from him. This word *disciple* has been used earlier in the gospels and included followers who were curious, counterfeit, and committed. However, in this gospel call, Jesus raises the bar, refining and sharpening the definition of what it means to be a true disciple of His. Therefore, we see that this is an evangelistic call on what it means to come to and follow Him in a salvific way or to be a true disciple of the Lord Jesus Christ.

What is most shocking is Jesus' statement at the end of verse 26. If anyone comes to Him in a salvific way and has a relationship and love that is over Him, He says, "He cannot be my disciple." Please note that Jesus doesn't say, "He may be able to be my disciple." No, Jesus says that such a person cannot be His disciple. *May* is a word of permission. *Cannot* is a word of ability. For those that find a loving relationship greater than Jesus, they cannot be His disciple. We could paraphrase this condition several ways to emphasize this point:

- If anyone comes to Me for salvation but loves his father, mother, wife children, brothers, or sisters more than me, he is not worthy to be My disciple.
- If anyone comes to Me and desires to enter the kingdom of God but loves his father, mother, wife, children, brothers, or sisters more than Me, He hates Me and cannot be My disciple.
- If anyone comes to Me and desires eternal life but loves his father, mother, wife, children, brothers, or sisters more than Me, he despises Me and is not worthy of Me.
- If anyone comes to Me and desires to enter through the narrow gate, but loves his father, mother, wife, children, brothers, or sisters more than Me, he is not able and is unworthy to be My disciple.

This is all to say that at salvation Jesus becomes the sum and substance of one's life. Jesus is the priority and everything else becomes the periphery. This is to say that a person who has decided to follow Christ will live a life that loves Jesus to the extent that, by comparison, it appears as hate toward others. This is to say that the true disciple of Christ cares more about what Christ thinks than their most cherished loved ones. The disciple of Christ will still love all those in his close concentric circle, but it will become clear to those in the close concentric circle that the true disciple's allegiance, loyalty, and love are given to the Lord Jesus Christ.

Sixth, we should see that one who is loving his own life more than Christ cannot be His disciple. It is as if Jesus is just pushing down His foot on the accelerator. If there was ever a chance to lighten His terms of discipleship, it would seem appropriate to do so now. However, Jesus only intensifies His call. Not only does

Jesus call for hating one's father, mother, wife, brothers, sisters, and children, He now calls for one to hate their own life. In fact, the word *life* comes from the original word *psuché*. As we learned earlier, *psuché* can mean "the human soul," "the soul as the seat of affections and will," "the self," or "a human person, an individual." Jesus certainly isn't calling for self-mutilation, suicide, or anything of the sort. So, what does it mean when one hates their own life or hates their own soul?

Once again, Jesus is purposefully creating extremes. He is pitting the affections of one's own life and soul against their affections to Him. Jesus says it this way in John 12:25 regarding hating one's life, "Whoever loves his life loses it, and whoever hates his life in the world will keep it for eternal life." This could easily be translated to say, "Whoever loves his soul loses it, and whoever hates his soul in the world will keep it for eternal life." As we noted earlier, the one who hates His own soul and forsakes it for the sake of Jesus is the one who saves it. You could simply love your own soul and be the lord of your own life but, in the end, you lose it for all eternity. This is a call to absolute devotion and love to the Lord Jesus Christ. It is not only hard to love Jesus above one's most loved ones, but now Jesus is calling for one's love and devotion to Him to be greater than the love for one's own life. This call demands a spiritual evaluation of one's life and whether one's personal interests, personal hobbies, personal sins, personal ambitions, and personal pursuits will take precedence, priority, and preeminence over Christ. It is a call to assess whether one loves their own lordship over their life or loves Christ preeminently. To *love Christ preeminently* is to say that Jesus' direction for your life is the driving force and not your own pursuits. The Lord Jesus Christ may choose to give His true disciples abundance and great wealth. However, He may also call for one to give everything, perhaps one's own life, for the sake of Him and His gospel.

Jesus reiterates this very same message in Matthew 10:39, where He says, "Whoever finds his life will lose it, and whoever loses his life for my sake will find it." To love one's own life over Christ is to despise Christ. To love one's own life over Christ is to hate Christ. The one who loves their own life over Christ will never deny themselves, pick up their cross, and come after Christ because they love their life too much to deny themselves. To love one's life over Christ is to worship the unholy trinity of me, myself, and I. We could paraphrase Christ's call to hate one's own life this way:

- If anyone comes to Me for salvation but loves being the lord of his life more than Me is not worthy to be My disciple.
- If anyone comes to Me and desires to enter the kingdom of God but loves his life more than Me and will not deny himself shows his hate for Me and cannot be My disciple.
- If anyone comes to Me and desires eternal life but loves his life more than Me, despises Me and is not worthy of Me.
- If anyone comes to Me and desires to enter through the narrow gate but loves his own soul and selfish desires more than Me is not able and is unworthy to be My disciple.

To come to Christ and not hate oneself or give Christ one's preeminent love is actually self-love that will not repent of sins, will not say goodbye to worldly desires, will not say goodbye to pride, will not say goodbye to self-will, will not say goodbye to self-righteousness, will not self-deny, and will not take Christ's yoke and learn from Him. To love the unholy trinity of me, myself, and I is to hate the Lord Jesus Christ. Once again, these are absolute terms. Christ will not take second place. Christ the Creator will not share preeminent love and loyalty with anything or anyone else for He is a jealous God (Exodus 34:14).

Luke 14:27—*Whoever does not carry his own cross and come after me cannot be my disciple*

Seventh, we should see that the one who does not pick up his own cross, or rather, die to himself and come after Christ, cannot be His disciple. So, not only does Jesus call for the preeminent love over every other relation, including the love of one's own life, Christ now calls for His true disciples to carry their own cross. As we learned earlier, to take up one's cross is a command to make a final decision to not only deny yourself and hate yourself, but to also die to yourself. Notice that this is not cross-wearing, it is cross-bearing. Bearing a cross 2,000 years ago had a very specific meaning. Bearing a cross meant strapping an instrument of death on your back. It was a walk of death that included disgrace, shame, pain, and persecution. Disgrace was guaranteed. Shame was promised. Pain was a certainty. Persecution was inevitable. Jesus was calling for a self-denying, self-hating, cross-bearing, Christ-identifying walk where a person would so identify with Him that they would do so even to the point of death. Notice in Luke's account that Christ says this cross-bearing would be daily (Luke 9:23). A cross-bearing death to self was to be the walk and manner of one's life. Cross-bearing was not glorious.

To come after Christ is the same thing as following Him (Matthew 16:24, Mark 8:34, Luke 9:23). To come after Christ is to listen to the Good Shepherd and follow Him (John 10:3–4). To come after Christ is to hear His words and practice them (Matthew 7:24–27, Luke 6:46–49). To come after Christ is to hear His words and keep them (Luke 11:28). To come after Christ is to listen to His commands and obey them (John 14:23, 15:10). To come after Christ is to be a *doulos* of Christ, which is where the *doulos* has no life of his own, no will of his own, no purpose of his own, and no plan of his own. All things are subject to his master. Every thought, breath, and effort are subject to the will of his master. The existence of the *doulos* was for the will and purpose of his master and nothing else. To come after Christ is to follow Christ with a submissive, self-denying, obedient, loving, and repentant faith.

This statement by Jesus would have been shocking. Just as one was to deny themselves, they were also called to repent and die to worldly desires, die to pride, die to self-will, die to self-sufficiency, die to self-wishes, die to self-righteousness, and die to themselves. They were to live for Christ's yoke, Christ's will, and Christ's rule over their life. This is a step of self-humiliation. This is a step of self-renunciation. Taking up one's cross is to die to self and surrender to the King of heaven, the Lord Jesus Christ. Is it possible to be a true disciple and follow after Christ without a faith that is submissive and obedient and that gives preeminent love to the Lord? Jesus does not think so. In fact, Jesus knows it is not possible where He says such a person "cannot be my disciple." To put it another way, Jesus said it this way in Matthew 10:38, "And whoever does not take his cross and follow me is not worthy of me."

Eighth, we should see that Jesus is making a claim to deity or to be God. There is nothing or no one in all creation that should have this kind of love and devotion other than God. As we recalled earlier, the greatest commandment by Jesus is the Shema and He reiterated this when asked what the greatest commandment is (Mark 12:28–34, 22:34–39). The Shema is found in Deuteronomy 6:4–5 and reads, "Hear, O Israel: The LORD our God, the LORD is one. You shall love the LORD your God with all your heart and with all your soul and with all your might." For Jesus Christ to turn to the crowd and call the crowd to love Him more than anyone else was a claim to deity and the people should have known this.

Ninth, Jesus spoke of this kind of love and inexpressible joy in coming to Him in saving faith in two parables. In Matthew 13:44–46, there are two parables: the Hidden Treasure and the Pearl. In Matthew 13:44, He says, "The kingdom of heaven is like treasure hidden in a field. When a man found it, he hid it again, and then in his joy went and sold all he had and bought the field." This is speaking of a man who finds Jesus Christ, the forgiveness of sins, eternal life, and reconciliation and a relationship with the Living God. The man is filled with joy inexpressible and sells everything to buy the field. This more specifically talks about the joy and price people are willing to pay to enter the kingdom of God. This is the most valuable possession in the world that is worth the cost of a personal cross, denying yourself, and submitting, and trusting in Christ. In Matthew 13:45–46, Jesus says, "Again, the kingdom of heaven is like a merchant looking for fine pearls. When he found one of great value, he went away and sold everything he had and bought it." There are differences in each parable, but the underlying theme is that those who have found the forgiveness of sins, Jesus Christ, and eternal life will pay the price because what they have found is so much more valuable than anything else in this life.

Luke 14:28–30—*For which of you, desiring to build a tower, does not first sit down and count the cost, whether he has enough to complete it? Otherwise, when he has laid a foundation and is not able to finish, all who see it begin to mock him, saying, 'This man began to build and was not able to finish.'*

Tenth, we should see that Jesus is calling people to count the cost to follow Him. He has laid down His terms for being His disciple. He is calling everyone to stop and consider the cost. He does not want a quick decision. He does not want to coerce anyone. He is not guaranteeing what will happen in the next five, ten, or twenty years. He is simply stating that you will need to carefully consider whether you're willing to commit to Him. In an ultimate shame and honor society, such as the Jewish culture, they would have understood this parable. They would know that it would be foolish to start to build a building without first determining whether they could finish. The one who had not carefully counted the costs and decided to build without considering the costs would ultimately face great shame. Is it worth losing your life to gain Jesus? Is hating your own soul, denying yourself, dying to yourself, taking up your own cross, and following Jesus worth it? Christ is calling for a serious spiritual assessment. Can you really and truly relate to Paul where he says in Acts 20:24, "But I do not account my life of any value nor as precious to myself, if only I may finish my course and the ministry that I received from the Lord Jesus, to testify to the gospel of the grace of God"? Can you really and truly relate to Paul in Philippians 3:7–9, where he says, "But whatever gain I had, I counted as loss for the sake of Christ. Indeed, I count everything as loss because of the surpassing worth of knowing Christ Jesus my Lord. For his sake I have suffered the loss of all things and count them as rubbish, in order that I may gain Christ and be found in him, not having a righteousness of my own that comes from the law, but that which comes through faith in Christ, the righteousness from God that depends on faith"? All those who have been justified by faith can relate to such self-denying, self-hating, cross-bearing faith in Christ.

Luke 14:31–32—*Or what king, going out to encounter another king in war, will not sit down and deliberate whether he is able with ten thousand to meet him who comes against him with twenty thousand? And if not, while the other is yet a great way off, he sends a delegation and asks for terms of peace.*

Eleventh, we should see that the King will return one day, and He will not be coming as the suffering servant, but as the conquering King. This King will come to judge and wage war (Revelation 19:11). This King will come with His armies (Revelation 19:14). This King will strike down nations with His Word (Revelation 19:15). This King will tread upon His enemies with the wrath of God (Revelation 19:15). This King will kill and destroy His enemies (Revelation 19:21). This King will come with a wrath so horrible that people will cry for mountains and rocks to fall on them rather than suffer the wrath of the Lamb (Revelation 6:16–17). This is the King that is coming, and He has made terms of peace. Jesus is saying that the king with 10,000 men should see that he is outnumbered and outmatched against the King with 20,000 men. This King will either say, "Well done, good and faithful slave" or "Bring them here and slaughter them before Me." This King will either say, "Enter into the joy of your master" or "Cast that worthless servant into outer darkness. In that place there will be weeping and gnashing of teeth." The King will either say, "Come, you who are blessed by my Father, inherit the kingdom prepared for you from the foundation of the world" or "Depart from Me, you cursed, into the eternal fire prepared for the devil and his angels." The King will either say, "Well done, good and faithful slave" or "Cut him in pieces and put him with the unfaithful." This King will either say, "Well done, good and faithful servant" or "You wicked and slothful slave, I never knew you, depart from Me you worker of lawlessness."

Jesus is stating that the king with 10,000 men should request terms of peace from the King with 20,000 men. Psalm 2 pictures this beautifully where the nations are seen raging against the LORD and against the One enthroned in heaven. At the end of Psalm 2, in verse 12, the psalmist says this, "Kiss the Son, lest he be angry, and you perish in the way, for his wrath is quickly kindled. Blessed are all who take refuge in him." Psalm 2:12 is a picture of someone coming to the throne and submitting to the LORD. The psalmist is picturing a dignitary receiving the humble kiss of an inferior submitting and pledging allegiance. In this very same way, the Lord Jesus Christ has given an invitation to submit to Him. The great banquet invitation has been issued. The terms of this invitation have been defined by the King of heaven for all mankind. You don't want to meet this King without agreeing to His terms of repentance and faith. You don't want to meet this King if you've created your own terms of peace. You don't want to meet this King relying on water baptism, confirmation, giving money to church, church membership, taking the Lord's Supper, good works, or any of the like for salvation. There is time to come to terms with this King for He is a good, gracious, kind, compassionate, forgiving, loving, and merciful King. If you come to this King on His terms of faith, He will forgive your sins and give you His righteousness. The transaction will be swift and instantaneous. This gracious King says, "Come now, let us reason together, though your sins are like scarlet, they shall be as white as snow; though they are red like crimson, they shall become like wool." (Isaiah 1:18). Come to this King and accept His invitation for you will find rest for your soul (Matthew 11:28–30) and grace in your time of need (Hebrews 4:16). Come to this King and receive His invitation into the kingdom of God and He will remember your sins no more (Hebrews 8:12).

Luke 14:33—*So therefore, any one of you who does not renounce all that he has cannot be my disciple.*

Twelfth, we should see that those who do not renounce all they have cannot be Christ's disciple. *Renounce* comes from the original word *apotassó* which means to "withdraw from," "renounce," or "send away." Properly, *apotassó* means "to say goodbye and depart from or to bid farewell, forsake, or send away." When Jesus calls for the renouncing of all one's possessions, He is now talking about possessions. As mentioned above, He may not ask you to give up everything, but you must be willing to give up everything if He calls you. In fact, in this life, He may give you an abundance or more than you need. However, He may require everything of you. Regardless of what He decides, are you willing to give up everything for Him? Therefore, Jesus Christ is calling you to become an owner of nothing and a steward of everything.

Thus, we see that Christ is asking for total allegiance and trust with your personal relationships, personal life, and possessions. This is the invitation to the great banquet. This is a gospel call for a submissive, preeminent loving faith in the Lord Jesus Christ and a relationship with Him. As in the parable of the Great Banquet, Christ called for an evaluation if you will lovingly submit to and trust in Him above land (Luke 14:18), possessions (Luke 14:19), and relationships (Luke 14:20).

Thirteenth, we can see what James would have in mind when he called his listeners to "draw near to God." They were to draw near to God on the Lord's terms and not their own. They were to draw near to God with their heart. They were to draw near to God through the Lord Jesus Christ. They were to draw near to God with a heart that submissively loved the Lord Jesus Christ with all one's heart, mind, soul, and strength. They were to draw near to God through the Lord Jesus Christ with a heart that loved Jesus Christ above all relationships, above one's own life, and above all material wealth and possessions. They were to draw near to God through the Lord Jesus Christ and give their life to Christ and follow Him wherever He leads. This is what James would have had in mind when He said, "Draw near to God."

Christ's Response to Those Who Draw Near

James 4:8—*Draw near to God, **and he will draw near to you**.*

This last statement by James describes the heart of the Lord for sinners. In Zechariah 1:3, the LORD says this to the Jews regarding His willingness to receive them back where He says, "Therefore say to them, thus declares the LORD of hosts: Return to me, says the LORD of hosts, and **I will return to you**, says the LORD of hosts." In Matthew 23:37, Jesus says this regarding His desire to care for Jerusalem where He says, "O Jerusalem, Jerusalem, the city that kills the prophets and stones those who are sent to it! How often would I have gathered your children together as a hen gathers her brood under her wings, and you were not willing!" God is gracious, kind, good, loving, merciful, and forgiving. He rejoices over repentant sinners/repentant sheep coming to Him. He is the one who seeks the lost sinner (Luke 19:10). Christ is the one who seeks and finds the lost sinner/lost sheep (Luke 15:1–7). Christ is joyful when He finds a lost sinner/lost sheep (Luke 15:5). God and the angels celebrate in heaven when the lost sinner/lost coin is led to repentance in Christ (Luke 15:7). God is the one who seeks and searches for the lost sinner/lost coin (Luke 15:8). God is the one who celebrates in heaven in front of the angels when a lost sinner/lost coin is found (Luke 15:9–10). God is the one who draws the lost sinner/lost son to Himself (Luke 15:17). God is the one who brings about repentance in the lost sinner/lost son (Luke 15:18–20). God is the one who sees the lost sinner/lost son a long way off and has compassion and runs after Him and embraces him with kisses (Luke 15:20). God is the one who is ready to forgive all sins, give His righteousness, give His inheritance, give His full forgiveness and pardon, give everything to the lost sinner/lost son and throw a celebration (Luke 15:22–24). God is the one who celebrates and restores the broken relationship between God and man (Luke 15:32).

When James is stating that "He will draw near to you," James has in mind the lavish grace of the Lord Jesus Christ. James has in mind that Christ will remove one's sins as far as the east is from the west (Psalm 103:12). James has in mind that Christ will tread one's iniquities underfoot and cast one's sins in the depths of the sea (Micah 7:19). James has in mind that Christ will *"ou mé"* or *"no, not"* remember your sins anymore (Hebrews 8:12). James has in mind that Christ is now your Shepherd (John 10:3–4, 11). James has in mind that Christ knows the sheep and His sheep knows Him (John 10:14). James has in mind that no one will ever snatch away God's sheep (John 10:28–30). James has in mind that Christ's sheep will be in a relationship with Him and will follow Him (John 10:3–4, 27). To say that "He will draw near to you" is to acknowledge that, at salvation, Christ will forgive your sins, make you His child, give you His righteousness, give you all He has, give you His guidance, give you His comfort, give you eternal life, give you the Holy Spirit, give you His wisdom, give you His nature, give you His blessing, and more. What in this world could be better than drawing near to God and having God draw near to you? Absolutely nothing! Once again, let us paraphrase James' command as we end this chapter:

"Draw near to God with your heart by loving the Lord Jesus Christ with all your heart, and with all your soul, and with all your mind, and with all your strength. Hate your father and mother and wife and children and brothers and sisters, yes and even your own life. Renounce all that you have, take up your cross and follow the Lord Jesus Christ and He will draw near to you and give you the free gift of eternal life that you may have fellowship with Him and with the Father."

CHAPTER 3

The Gospel Call for Repentant Faith: Turning Away from Sin and toward the Lord Jesus Christ

James 4:8—*Cleanse your hands, you sinners, and purify your hearts, you double-minded*

The fourth and fifth aorist imperatives and characteristics of saving faith that James gives is to "cleanse your hands" and "purify your hearts." The word *cleanse* comes from *katharizó* and means to "make clean" or "cleanse ceremonially or spiritually." Properly, it means "to make pure by removing all admixture or intermingling of filth." The word *purify* comes from *hagnizó* which means to "cleanse from defilement" or "cleanse ceremonially or morally." *Hagnizó* describes what is "morally undefiled" and, when used ceremonially, describes "that which has been so cleansed that it is fit to be brought into the presence of God and used in His service." Both words have strong connections to Jewish ceremonial washing.

For example, in Exodus 30:19, there are instructions for handwashing when the priests were to enter the tent of meeting where it says:

*"You shall also make a basin of bronze, with its stand of bronze, for washing. You shall put it between the tent of meeting and the altar, and you shall put water in it, with which Aaron and his sons **shall wash their hands and their feet.** When they go into the tent of meeting, or when they come near the altar to minister, to burn a food offering to the Lord, they shall wash with water, so that they may not die. **They shall wash their hands and their feet**, so **that they may not die**. It shall be a statute forever to them, even to him and to his offspring throughout their generations."*

Here we see that the washing of hands and feet was to be symbolic. The priests were to wash their hands and feet before they entered the LORD's presence as the hands symbolized what the priests did and their feet symbolized where they went. In essence, this would allow the priests to see the sins they committed with their hands and the sins they committed wherever they went. This symbolism was to help the priests see the need for a repentant, contrite, and God-fearing heart before they were to enter the presence of the LORD. A lack of *ritual cleanliness*, or unwashed hands and feet, would be an offense worthy of death. Such a punishment for not taking one's sins seriously and appearing before the LORD with unwashed and ceremonially defiled hands would be worthy of death.

The Israelites would surely know of what James meant by having hands that sin and how the LORD rejected worship when one was outwardly and unrepentantly committing sin where the LORD says this in Isaiah 1:15–17, "When you spread out **your hands**, I will hide my eyes from you; even though you make many prayers, I will not listen; **your hands** are full of blood. **Wash yourselves**; make yourselves **clean**; remove the evil of your deeds from before my eyes; cease to do evil, learn to do good; seek justice, correct oppression; bring justice to the fatherless, plead the widow's cause." Here we see that the LORD was calling for repentance. The LORD was not pleased with prayers and worship from a worshipper that was unrepentant and practicing the very things He hates. The LORD wasn't calling for an external washing, but rather, a repentance that turns from shedding blood and practicing evil to learning good, seeking justice, and helping those in need.

Not only would the Israelites know that repentance would turn away from practicing evil with their hands and feet, they would also know that there was a heart repentance. Isaiah 55:6–7 captures such a repentance for one's outward sinful works as well as an inward repentance where the LORD says, "Seek the Lord while he may be found; call upon him while he is near; **let the wicked <u>forsake his way</u>, and the unrighteous man his thoughts**; let him <u>return</u> to the Lord**, that he may have compassion on him, and to our God, for he will abundantly pardon." When James was calling for one to purify their hearts, the Jews would know that He was calling for heart transformation, heart repentance, or rather, a heart circumcision. In Deuteronomy 10:12–16, the LORD called for a circumcised heart where He says:

*"And now, Israel, **what does the Lord your God require of you, but to <u>fear</u> the Lord your God, to <u>walk</u> in all his ways, to <u>love</u> him, to <u>serve</u> the Lord your God with all your heart and with all your soul, and to keep the commandments and statutes of the Lord,** which I am commanding you today for your good? Behold, to the Lord your God belong heaven and the heaven of heavens, the earth with all that is in it. Yet the Lord set his heart in love on your fathers and chose their offspring after them, you above all peoples, as you are this day. **<u>Circumcise</u> therefore the foreskin of your heart,** and be no longer stubborn."*

We can see that a heart that was purified was a circumcised heart that was repentant and was no longer stubborn. Deuteronomy 10:12 basically gives the definition of a *circumcised, regenerate, and converted heart*. Conversely, an *uncircumcised heart* was an unpurified heart that was unrepentant, disobedient, self-willed, unconverted, and rebellious toward the LORD. The LORD gave this same command for a repentant and purified heart to Judah and Jerusalem in Jeremiah 4:4, where He says, "Circumcise yourselves to the Lord; remove the foreskin of your hearts."

Additionally, the circumcised heart was one that had been circumcised by the LORD (Deuteronomy 30:6). The LORD was the one who circumcised the foreskin of the heart, and the circumcised heart was a God-fearing, obedient, submissive, God-loving, and God-serving repentant heart. David captures the repentant, heart-circumcised, hand-purified, and heart-cleansed person who could enter into the LORD's presence where he says this in Psalm 24:3, "Who may ascend the mountain of the LORD? Who may stand in his holy place? The one who has **clean hands** and a **pure heart**, who does not trust in an idol or swear by a false god."

Furthermore, Jeremiah gives a call to repentance in Lamentations to Judah that speaks of repentance with one's heart and hands. In Lamentations 3:41-42 he says, "Let us lift up our **hearts** and **hands** to God in heaven: 'We have transgressed and rebelled, and you have not forgiven.'" Judah was called to repent from the heart and turn away from their sins, stop committing the very sins that brought judgment upon their nation, and return to the LORD.

When James is giving the aorist imperatives to "cleanse your hands, you sinners, and purify your hearts, you double-minded," he is giving a call to true repentance. In fact, when James calls his listeners "sinners" and "double-minded," we can be sure that he is giving a gospel invitation to the unconverted. The word *sinners* comes from *hamartólos* which means "sinning," "sinful," "depraved," or "detestable." This word means "to miss the mark which is God's divine standard or law." Properly, it is "someone who is continually erring from the way and living in opposition to God's good and acceptable and perfect will." This adjective expresses the idea of moral wickedness and consequent exposure to divine displeasure. The word *double-minded* comes from *dipsuchos* which means "two-souled" or "two-minded." It is used to describe a person who is split in half and is like a spiritual schizophrenic. It is an adjective used to describe one who is two-faced with God and has wavering inconsistency. Such a person vacillates between two or more opinions and has divided loyalty which is manifest by indecision and doubting. Such a man tries to be friends with the world and a friend with God. Such a man who is double-minded has an adulterous, unconverted, unregenerate, and unsaved heart (James 4:4). Therefore, we can know that such a person who is marked by outright sin and double-mindedness is not saved.

So, what kind of hand-cleansing, heart-purifying repentance would James have in mind? Is there an example of a preacher that preached repentance with force, boldness, clarity, and conviction? Perhaps it would be beneficial to understand how the forerunner to Jesus preached repentance. Perhaps it would be beneficial to understand how the half-brother of Jesus understood Christ's statement of John the Baptist who preached a baptism of repentance for the forgiveness of sins where He said, "Truly, I say to you, among those born of women there has arisen no one greater than John the Baptist" (Matthew 11:11). Perhaps it would be beneficial to see John the Baptist's theology on repentance as James undoubtedly heard John the Baptist's preaching on repentance (Acts 11) and heard Jesus preach repentance with just as much force, boldness, clarity, and conviction as John the Baptist (Matthew 4:17).

The Baptism of Repentance for the Forgiveness of Sins

John the Baptist had an extraordinary ministry. John the Baptist was the son of a priest named Zechariah who belonged to the priestly division of Abijah. John's mother was Elizabeth, who was also a descendant of Aaron. Elizabeth was related to Mary, the mother of Jesus, so John the Baptist would have also been related to Jesus. John was the forerunner to Jesus and had the ministry of getting the nation of Israel ready for the Messiah and preparing the way of the Lord. John's ministry was to bring back many of the people of Israel to the Lord their God and to turn the hearts of the parents to their children and the disobedient to the wisdom of the righteous—to make ready a people prepared for the Lord (Luke 1:17). John was to go before the Lord in the spirit and power of Elijah, which means he would be known for being bold and uncompromising in his stand for the Word of God (Luke 1:17). To understand how John was to turn the hearts of the people and make ready a people for the Lord, let us look at how John did this as he preached a baptism of repentance for the forgiveness of sins in Luke 3.

Luke 3:3—*He went into all the country around the Jordan, preaching a baptism of repentance for the forgiveness of sins.*

John begins his ministry preaching a baptism of repentance. Let's stop and pause to understand *"preached a baptism of repentance."* The first word to observe is *preached*. *Preached* is translated from *kérussó* which means "to herald, to proclaim, and to preach a message publicly and with conviction and persuasion." The second word to understand is *repentance*. In the original language, the word is *metanoia*. *Metanoia* means "a change of mind." This changing of the mind is not mere intellectual assent, but it also impacts the emotional affections and the volitional will of man.

John's ministry was one of confrontation with the nation of Israel. It was not only a call to national repentance, but also a call to personal repentance. In ancient times, the herald would go before a king and announce the king's message. The herald would come with the king's message and whether it was an order for the nation's surrender or an edict from the king, the messenger would go throughout the towns and villages and announce the king's message. The herald would not be quiet. The herald would bring forth the message with conviction and all authority of the king. The herald would neither dare to misrepresent the king's message, add to the king's message, leave anything out from the king's message, nor would the herald quietly announce the message. In fact, in ancient times, the herald was to announce the message with a gravity and authority that required the listeners to obey. The herald was not to enter negotiations. The herald was to learn the message and speak the message with the force and conviction of the king himself. The herald would boldly, loudly, and clearly articulate the message of the king to all people with conviction. John the Baptist was no different. His job was to boldly, loudly, and clearly articulate the message with the conviction of the Lord to repent and be baptized. His message was not just a mere change of mind, but a call to prepare one's heart and life to turn away from sin and toward the Messiah. His job was to proclaim that all of Israel needed to repent and be baptized for the forgiveness of sins. He did not enter negotiations. He did not change the King's message. He was not *a reed swayed by the wind,* meaning that he was not a weak man with no convictions (Matthew 11:7). He was a herald and preacher of repentance. The next question that arises is what did this baptism of repentance represent?

There were several ceremonial washings in the Old Testament. However, there was a specific meaning behind John's baptism that would have been especially offensive. Under the old covenant, there was a ceremonial ablution or washing for Gentiles who would convert to Judaism. This ceremonial washing of proselytes was considered purification from heathenism and an initiation or consecration of the convert before his admission to the people of God. Since a Gentile had lived in what was considered heathen pollution and was also considered a heathen and impure, the Gentile would be required to complete a purification process to fully become an Israelite. It was, thus, required of every Gentile to submit to the rite of purification from heathen pollution by immersion. The Babylonian Talmud says that, concerning proselytes, "one is not to be regarded as a proselyte until he has been circumcised and undergone immersion, and as long as he has not undergone immersion, he is still a non-Jew." This was a part of rabbinic regulations for ceremonial purifications and required three witnesses. The candidate, if a male, was first circumcised and when the wound had healed, he was taken to the bath. While he stood in the water, the rabbis once more recited to him some of the great and lesser commandments. The convert would then make a complete immersion and stepped forth as a fully privileged Israelite. In addition to this, the proselyte would be asked questions such as, "What makes thee desire to become a proselyte?" and, if the proselyte would answer, "I am not worthy to give my neck to the yoke of Him who spoke the word and the world came into existence," they would immediately accept him and move forward with the baptism while also reciting commandments.

John's baptism of repentance was a proselyte baptism of repentance for Israel. In other words, John was proclaiming to them with full gravity and conviction that they were not ready for the Messiah. John was telling them that they needed to see themselves as Gentiles. John was telling them that they needed to see themselves as unrighteous as tax collectors, prostitutes, swindlers, whoremongers, fornicators, and outright sinners. John was telling them that their circumcision meant nothing in terms of salvation. John was telling them that their ancestry meant nothing in terms of salvation. John was telling them that their religious rituals meant nothing in terms of salvation. John was telling them that their good works meant nothing in terms of salvation. John was telling them that they were not ready for the Messiah and, if they wanted to receive forgiveness of sins that could be offered by the Messiah, they would need to consider themselves as Gentiles. John was telling them that if they wanted forgiveness of sins as offered by the Messiah, they should consider themselves outside of God's covenant people, that they should consider themselves cut off from God, that they should consider themselves ceremonially unclean to accept the Messiah, that they should consider themselves as equals with the Gentile pagan, and that they should consider themselves unrighteous and damned. This was the meaning of John's baptism of repentance for the forgiveness of sins.

It would have been an extreme shock to the Jews who thought they were the covenant people and were righteous. This message would have turned their world upside down as John not only commanded all of Israel to repent and identify as a Gentile, even the religious leaders and teachers of Judaism were called to this very same repentance. No one in the nation of Israel was excluded from the command to be baptized, repent, identify as a Gentile, confess their sins, and throw themselves at the mercy of the Messiah. This was an extreme message for the Jews to prepare for the Messiah's coming and it was a radical call to turn not only nationally, but also personally, to the Messiah. Isaiah 1:5–6 captures the state of where Israel was just prior to the Messiah's coming where it says, 'Why should you be beaten anymore? Why do you persist in rebellion? Your whole head is injured, your whole heart afflicted. From the sole of your foot to the top of your head there is no soundness—only wounds and welts and open sores, not cleansed or bandaged or soothed with olive oil." John proclaimed this very same message to the Jews. They were unsound from the top of their head to the sole of their foot.

Luke 3:4–6—*As it is written in the book of the words of Isaiah the prophet: "A voice of one calling in the wilderness, 'Prepare the way for the Lord, make straight paths for him. Every valley shall be filled in, every mountain and hill made low. The crooked roads shall become straight, the rough ways smooth. And all people will see God's salvation.'"*

John the Baptist has just quoted from Isaiah 40. Although the message and baptism of repentance would have been shocking and offensive as it called for a radical spiritual repentance, John was also citing a promise from Isaiah where God comforts His people. In Isaiah 40, God announces comfort for His people (v. 1), God has said that Jerusalem's penalty has been paid for twice over (v. 2), God promises to tend to His flock like a shepherd (v. 11), God declares His sovereignty and power (v. 15–25), and promises hope for those who trust in Him (29–31). John is preparing Israel to receive their Messiah and he begins to explain repentance through Isaiah 40:3–5.

John's theology of repentance according to Isaiah starts with, "Prepare the way for the Lord, make straight paths for him." John is not calling for a massive demolition and construction of a physical path or road. No, his ministry was to prepare the hearts of the people (Luke 1:17). Therefore, in this short little sentence John is saying that any obstacles that would deter the people from accepting the Messiah must be put away. John is saying that every person needs to clean out their spiritual closet. He is saying that everyone in Israel needs to get rid of their apathy, get rid of their pride, get rid of their distractions, get rid of false religion, get rid of other priorities that interfere with God, get rid of self-reliance, get rid of hypocrisy, get rid of self-will, and get rid of anything that is going to prevent them from accepting the Messiah.

He goes on to state that the crooked roads shall become straight, the rough ways smooth. Once again, John wasn't calling for a road construction project. John was calling for a total self-evaluation. In verse 5, he said, "Every valley shall be filled in, every mountain and hill made low." When John said that *"every valley shall be filled in,"* he was stating that every sin shall be brought up and openly confessed. Take your sins and confess them and do not hold anything back. All the debase sins that you cherish shall be raised up and elevated so that you may be brought low and humbled to receive the Messiah. Notice that he says *"every."* This was a radical repentance. He was saying that the sins that the people knew about in their lives needed to be confessed and rejected. He was saying that all the hidden sins in the valley of one's heart needed to be exposed. Likewise, John said that "every mountain and hill needed to be brought low." He's stating that every righteous act and that every self-exalting accomplishment must be brought low. There was no room for confidence in circumcision. There was no room for confidence in ceremonial washing. There was no room for confidence in Sabbath observance-keeping. He's saying that your sins must be elevated, all your good deeds and religious accomplishments brought low, and every other obstacle in your life must be dealt with and removed. There was no room for religious exaltation, only room for soul-searching repentance and humility and a heart readiness to accept the Messiah as Lord and Savior.

Luke 3:7–8—*John said to the crowds coming out to be baptized by him, "You, brood of vipers! Who warned you to flee from the coming wrath? Produce fruit in keeping with repentance. And do not begin to say to yourselves, 'We have Abraham as our father.' For I tell you that out of these stones God can raise up children for Abraham."*

So, as John is performing his ministry of preparing the nation of Israel for the Messiah, he is also confronting people that do not have true repentance. Here, he calls them "a brood of vipers." Notice that he doesn't call them "Abraham's descendants." He doesn't call them "children of God." He doesn't call them "sons of Israel." No, he calls them a *"brood of vipers."* He is calling them "children of serpents." In Matthew's account, he is speaking specifically with Sadducees and Pharisees, but, in Luke's account, Luke makes no distinction and includes the crowds. He is not calling them "covenant people of God," but "children of the devil." He is warning Israel of divine wrath and judgment. The people of Israel would have picked up on this. They would have known of the serpent in Genesis 3. They would have known that John was telling them they were still under divine wrath and judgment. Notice too that he tells this to the religious Israelites. Israel should have known better that entrance into the kingdom was not a group affair but an individual entrance into the kingdom. They would have known Psalm 1:1–2, "Blessed is the one who does not walk in step with the wicked or stand in the way of sinners or sit in the seat of scoffers, but whose delight is in the law of the LORD, and who meditates on His law day and night." They would have known that this should have been an individual repentance and not just another ritual.

Notice as well that he says, "Who warned you to flee from the coming wrath?" This wrath isn't the wrath of the devil or the wrath of demons or the wrath of men. No, true repentance is an understanding that one is fleeing from the wrath and judgment of God. In other words, John is saying, "So you heard that there was a baptism of repentance and now you're looking to go through a ceremonial rite or ritual to escape God's wrath. Don't do that! Don't think that divine judgment will not fall on you just because you've been baptized. Don't presume that the Jordan River will make you right with God." John further goes on to refine what repentance should look like when he says, "Produce fruit in keeping with repentance." As we learned earlier, the word *worthy* comes from *axios* and it means "to weigh in keeping with how something weighs in on God's balance-scale of truth." In other words, John is telling them that this ritual means nothing, but what means everything is the heart preparation as it relates to repentance. If the people of Israel do see their offense toward God, have intellectual knowledge of their sins, understand they have no merit before God, mourn over their status before God, and humble themselves to obey God and receive the Messiah, they should bring forth fruit that God finds worthy of repentance. If there is no fruit of repentance, there was never a root of true repentance, but rather, a false repentance and dead ritual. John's call for repentance doesn't only apply to the people of Israel, but also applies to all people today. God commands all men everywhere to repent (Acts 17:30).

John was very concerned about false repentance. John knew how wicked the heart was and how man would want the easy road. John knew that not everyone who came to be baptized for repentance would bear fruits of repentance. John was preparing the people for the Messiah and was trying to warn them of a repentance that bore no true fruit. A repentance that bears no fruit is a *dead repentance*. A repentance that doesn't elevate the sins is a *dead repentance*. A repentance that doesn't bring one's pride and righteous accomplishments down low is a *dead repentance*. A repentance that does no soul searching to remove spiritual obstacles from the heart is a *dead repentance*.

John's theology on man's heart would have surely been solid. Surely, John would have known that the heart of a man in its natural state was desperately wicked (Jeremiah 17:9), perverse (Proverbs 11:20), evil (Genesis 6:5), full of madness (Ecclesiastes 9:3), unwashed (Jeremiah 4:14), deceitful and deceived (Jeremiah 17:9), disloyal (Psalm 78:37), straying (Proverbs 7:25), impenitent (Deuteronomy 10:16), unbelieving (Hebrews 3:12), hard (Zechariah 7:12), proud (Proverbs 16:5), covetous (Jeremiah 22:17), murderous (Jeremiah 22:17), foolish (Proverbs 14:1), idolatrous (Ezekiel 14:3), rebellious (Jeremiah 5:23), stubborn (Jeremiah 18:12), and dull (Isaiah 6:10). The job of John was to shock the Jews out of cardiac arrest and bring about a true heart repentance.

In verse 8, he says, "And do not begin to say to yourselves, 'We have Abraham as our father.' For I tell you that out of these stones God can raise up children for Abraham." John is making quite a statement here. He knows that the Jews are inclined to say they are the covenant children of God based on their national heritage. He knows that they are going to say they are circumcised and have the covenant sign. He knows that they are going to say they have the law of Moses, the Levitical system, and more. However, John is telling them not to presume you are righteous just because of your affiliation. Don't presume that because you're a born Israelite that you have right standing with God. Don't presume to say that because you're a priest and have been circumcised that you are eternally blessed by God.

Likewise, John's message bears weight today. Today's message to the church would be to say, "Don't presume because you've had a Christian baptism that you're going to heaven. Don't presume because you've made a profession of faith that you have eternal life or the Son. Don't presume because you've gone through confirmation that you have saving faith. Don't presume that because you're a part of a church that teaches biblical and orthodox doctrine that you are in the kingdom of God. No. Rather, you "need to produce fruit worthy of repentance."

Additionally, in verse 8, he says God is able from these stones to raise up children for Abraham. Once again, this was a hard and demeaning message. He has just gotten done calling them snakes and now he is saying that their position is no better than dirt. John is not calling them God's covenant people. He is saying that God can raise up dirt from the ground to be sons of Abraham. No doubt that this would have been incredibly offensive to the nation of Israel, but John's message of repentance was radical and demanded the people's heart be prepared for the Messiah.

Luke 3:9—*The ax is already at the root of the trees, and every tree that does not produce good fruit will be cut down and thrown into the fire.*

John is exhorting the Israelites to earnestly repent, but there is another element to repentance. Notice that John says, "The ax is already at the root of the trees." He is speaking of the urgency of needing to repent. The Israelites would have known what it meant for *the ax to be at the root of the tree*. This means that the one who is chopping down the tree only has one more swing of the ax before the tree falls. His ax has chopped away the bark and made it through the pulp and, now, there's only one more swing that will complete the fall of the tree. John was speaking of the urgency to repent. Not only had he clarified the nature of repentance, but now he was emphasizing the urgency of repentance. Don't wait one more day. Don't put this off. As John had referenced Isaiah 40, surely the people would have also remembered Isaiah 40:6–8, "All people are like grass, and all their faithfulness is like the flowers of the field. The grass withers and the flowers fall, because the breath of the LORD blows on them. Surely the people are grass. The grass withers and the flowers fall, but the word of our God endures forever." Surely, they would have known that time was of the essence in repentance. Jesus had also emphasized the point of urgently repenting when, in Luke 13:6–9, He gives a parable of a fig tree that has been given care for three years but has shown no fruit. While the man who was growing the fig tree was patient for three years, He gave it one more year to bear fruit otherwise He would cut it down. So, it is today that we must exhort men to repent. We can ascend no higher than John. We have no better message than what John, Jesus, or the apostles said. All men must repent and bear fruit worthy of repentance for their time on earth is short.

The next point John brings up is that a man that bears no fruit of repentance is not saved. The man that says he believes but produces no good fruit of repentance is an unbeliever and is unsaved. The destiny of a man who bears no fruit of repentance is evidence that the man was never regenerated. It is evidence that this man never had saving faith. The end of this man is an eternal punishment of fire in hell. Let's also stop and pause to note that John says *"every"* tree that does not produce good fruit is cut down. There is no exception to this. Either a man bears fruits of repentance or he doesn't.

We also see that this fire is an unquenchable fire. In verse 17, He says that His winnowing fork is in His hand to clear His threshing floor and to gather the wheat into His barn, but He will burn up the chaff with unquenchable fire. Once again, John is saying that time is of the essence. The farmer is separating the wheat and the chaff. The wheat has already been harvested. It is no longer growing season, but it is now a time of separation. The wheat is brought into the *barn,* which refers to believers, but the *chaff,* which represents unbelievers, is burned up with unquenchable fire. In those days, the people would have known what John was talking about with "burning the chaff with unquenchable fire." They lived in an agricultural community. The people would have known that when you burn chaff the fire will eventually subside as it runs out of substrate and is quenched. However, John's theology on hell and eternal punishment lines right up with Jesus' theology on hell. Note that John says that *the chaff will be burned up with unquenchable fire,* which means that the fires of hell go on for all eternity. This is a fire that never diminishes, but rather, burns as a raging furnace. This was a fire that would not go out once it had consumed the chaff. No, this fire would persist forever. This fire would not go out. The fire would never be quenched. The chaff would never stop burning. A man that bears no fruit of repentance is on his way to an unquenchable fire that will never go out. Let us etch this in our minds that the Gospel contains many elements, but it must always include divine wrath, divine judgment, and repentance. Often, we are too quick to say, "Put your faith in Jesus Christ and you will be saved." Let us learn from John that although the Gospel also includes an explanation of the person and work of Christ as well as the subjective elements of human response (i.e., faith), a faithful gospel preacher never leaves out divine wrath, divine judgment, and repentance as he warns men and calls them to Jesus Christ.

Luke 3:10–11—*"What should we do then?" the crowd asked. John answered, "Anyone who has two shirts should share with the one who has none, and anyone who has food should do the same."*

John continues to expound on his theology of repentance. Notice that John notes what true repentance will look like on the horizontal level or, rather, toward man. True repentance will love your neighbor as yourself. John would certainly have in mind Leviticus 19:18, "Do not seek revenge or bear a grudge against anyone among our people but love your neighbor as yourself. I am the LORD." John is saying that true repentance will show itself in loving your neighbor and meeting your neighbor's needs. He explains that there is not only a negative side to repentance, which is turning away from sin, but also a positive side to repentance, which is turning to righteousness that shows itself in acts of love that the LORD commands. Likewise, James describes a faith that saves and a faith that does not save. James describes a faith that has no care of meeting a neighbor's needs and concludes that a faith that cares nothing for his neighbor and cannot meet his neighbor's essential needs is a *dead faith (James 2:14–17)*.

Also, notice in verse 10 that the crowd says, "What should we do then?" Perhaps this was an honest question. Perhaps the crowd was indeed earnest to know what they needed to do. However, one ominous note here is that they needed to ask what to do rather than being deeply convicted. Perhaps they were asking out of deep conviction, but perhaps they really had no conviction at all and were blind to their sins. The main point is that if your sins are brought up to you, confess them, ask for forgiveness, ask for God's help to deliver you from the sin, and repent.

Luke 3:12–14—*Even tax collectors came to be baptized. "Teacher," they asked, "what should we do?" "Don't collect any more than you are required to," he told them. Then some soldiers asked him, "And what should we do?" He replied, "Don't extort money and don't accuse people falsely—be content with your pay."*

Here, John is expounding even more on true repentance. Here, John tells the tax collectors to be honest in their work and stop stealing. He tells soldiers not to steal and slander. John is talking about the negative side of repentance, which is the aspect of turning from sin. This is further highlighting Leviticus 19:18, which calls us to love our neighbor as ourselves. If we keep this command, we will not only positively love them by doing good to them, but we will also react in a negative sense where we will stop sinning against our neighbor. Not only this, but look at the flow of John's theology of repentance. He first explains that there is divine judgment and wrath coming in verses 7–9, which could be considered a vertical repentance toward God, but then also talks about a horizontal aspect of repentance toward men. This is how we must present repentance to all men. We must warn men of the wrath of God that is coming. We must warn men that they must turn from their sin and turn to Christ in faith for salvation. We should also explain that all men must turn from their personal sin against God, but also sinning against man. John's theology on baptism of repentance for the forgiveness of sins was thorough and complete.

Luke 3:15–17—*The people were waiting expectantly and were all wondering in their hearts if John might possibly be the Messiah. John answered them all, "I baptize you with water. But one who is more powerful than I will come, the straps of whose sandals I am not worthy to untie. He will baptize you with the Holy Spirit and fire. His winnowing fork is in his hand to clear his threshing floor and to gather the wheat into his barn, but he will burn up the chaff with unquenchable fire."*

As we mentioned earlier, John is saying that the time of tilling, planting, growing, and harvesting is already done. The farmer has the wheat on his threshing floor. The farmer is throwing the wheat and chaff in the air to separate the two components. The chaff, which is lighter, will blow away and the wheat will fall in the same place. The separation is already occurring. Although there is debate over what *baptize with the Holy Spirit and fire* means, it is helpful to understand this verse in context. In context, to be baptized with the Holy Spirit indicates that this baptism ultimately ends in salvation and would refer to the wheat that is brought into the barn. On the other hand, the baptism of fire should be tied to the chaff as the chaff is ultimately burned up with fire, thus *baptism of fire*. In other words, you are either baptized with the Holy Spirit and saved or baptized with fire and judged unto condemnation. Only Jesus can baptize with the Holy Spirit and save man and He alone can judge men and send them to hell. Thus, true repentance turns away from sin and toward Jesus in faith. Additionally, we should also see that John the Baptist was continually telling the people that he could only baptize with water, that he was not the Messiah, and only the Messiah could baptize with the Holy Spirit and fire. John was very careful to point away from himself as the Messiah and toward Jesus who was the Messiah (John 1:29). We won't have time to fully develop the understanding of the definition of the *Holy Spirit* so, in lieu of this, a definition of *baptism with the Holy Spirit* could be understood as follows: **The baptism with the Holy Spirit is the sovereign monergistic work of salvation performed by God the Father, God the Son, and God the Holy Spirit. The Holy Spirit is given from the Father to the Son (John 14:16, 15:26; Luke 11:13) and the Son pours out or gives the Holy Spirit in the Father's name (Matthew 3:11–12; Mark 1:8; Luke 3:16, 24:49; John 1:31–33; 14:16, 26; 15:26;**

16:7; Acts 1:4–5, 2:17–18, 10:44–48, 11:16, Titus 3:6). The Holy Spirit then regenerates or causes man to be born again (John 3:3–10, Titus 3:5, Ezekiel 36:25–27) through hearing the Word of God/Gospel (James 1:18, Ephesians 1:13, Romans 1:15–17, 10:17, 1 Corinthians 1:21) which gives spiritual life to the previously spiritually dead man (Ephesians 2:1–3, Colossians 2:13). God then grants man the ability to repent which is a gift (Acts 11:18, 2 Timothy 2:25) and put saving faith in Jesus Christ which is also a gift (Ephesians 2:8–9, Philippians 1:29, John 7:38–39). Man is then justified by grace through faith in Christ (Titus 3:7), receives and is indwelt by the Holy Spirit (Galatians 3:2, 3:14; Ephesians 1:13; 1 Corinthians 6:19), and the Holy Spirit spiritually unites/immerses man with Jesus Christ and puts the man into the body of Christ (1 Corinthians 12:13, Romans 6:3–4). Baptism with the Holy Spirit is not water baptism, and water baptism is not baptism with the Holy Spirit for only Christ can baptize with the Holy Spirit and man can only baptize with water (Matthew 3:11–12; Mark 1:8; Luke 3:16; John 1:31–33, 3:8, 7:38–39, 14:15–17, 26; 15:26, 16:7; Acts 1:4–5, 2:17–18, 10:44–48, 11:16; 1 Corinthians 1:17). Baptism with the Holy Spirit is a one-time, instantaneous, and salvific work of God (1 Corinthians 12:13).

In John's baptism of repentance for the forgiveness of sins, it would be a colossal mistake to think that the ritual of baptism is what forgave sins. John's message of repentance was radical, and John even warned against treating this baptism of repentance as just another ritual or ceremony. John was calling for heart-searching repentance that would bear fruit. If there was no fruit of repentance, but only a baptism, John would have warned that the person who went through the baptism was chaff that was just waiting to be burned with unquenchable fire. A person that desired to confess and reject his sins, reject his spiritual accomplishments, and getting rid of the barriers of the heart in preparation for the Messiah would have been characterized as wheat according to John.

As John's ministry is winding down, his disciples are noting that people are now following Jesus and not him. John humbly answers them this way in John 3:27, "A person cannot receive even one thing unless it is given him from heaven," which is an acknowledgment that John's ministry was simply given to him by the Lord. It was John's time to fade away and time for Christ's ministry to begin. John saw himself as a friend to the bridegroom or as a friend of Christ and then says this about the importance of Christ in John 3:30, "He must increase, but I must decrease." Finally, John ends with this statement about Jesus in John 3:36, "Whoever believes in the Son has eternal life; whoever does not obey the Son shall not see life, but the wrath of God remains on him." John saw that Jesus was the Son of God (John 3:36). John believed in the Triune Godhead (John 3:34–35). John believed that Jesus was the Christ (John 3:28–36). John believed that one must repent to accept the Messiah (Luke 3:3–18). John believed that if one did not believe in Jesus Christ the wrath of God remained on the one who remained in unbelief (John 3:36).

So, what did James have in mind when he gave the aorist imperatives to *"cleanse your hands"* and *"purify your hearts"*? James would have undoubtably had in mind a repentance of the heart (purified heart) that elevated the valleys or, rather, elevated one's sins to confess and repent of them and brought down the mountains and refused to acknowledge any spiritual accomplishments and would humble oneself before the Lord. Such a repentance of the heart would lead to bearing fruits of repentance, turning away from sin (cleansing hands), and an embrace of the Messiah. Let's remember that John the Baptist's hard message of repentance is part of the good news as it says in Luke 3:18, "So with many other exhortations he preached good news to the people." James would know that there is no gospel without repentance. James would clearly understand that a gospel with no repentance is no gospel at all. Let's keep this in mind as we transition to understand how James would be impacted by Jesus' preaching on repentance.

Christ's Preaching on Repentance

As John the Baptist's ministry was winding down, Jesus' ministry was starting. Mark records this in Mark 1:14–15 about Jesus' ministry, "Now after John was arrested, Jesus came into Galilee, proclaiming the gospel of God, and saying, 'The time is fulfilled, and the kingdom of God is at hand; repent and believe in the gospel.'" So, just as John's ministry started with a call to repent and embrace and believe in the Messiah, Jesus' ministry picked up right where John the Baptist's ministry finished. Jesus continually preached a message of repentance and belief in the gospel. In fact, Jesus gave present tense imperative commands to both repent and believe the good news. It is as if Jesus could even say it this way, "Repent and spend the rest of your life repenting. Believe the good news and spend the rest of your life believing the good news." When Jesus preached repentance, let's keep in mind that it would have carried the same gravity, boldness, and urgency as that of John the Baptist.

As Jesus started His ministry, His first sermon was given to His hometown of Nazareth on the Sabbath Day in the synagogue. He opened the scroll to Isaiah 61 and read the following in Luke 4:18–19, "The Spirit of the Lord is upon me, because he has anointed me to proclaim good news to the poor. He has sent me to proclaim liberty to the captives and recovering of sight to the blind, to set at liberty those who are oppressed, to proclaim the year of the Lord's favor." As Jesus rolled up the scroll, He said this in Luke 4:21, "Today this Scripture has been fulfilled in your hearing."

This would have been quite a statement and shock to the synagogue of Nazareth with Jesus' exposition of Isaiah 61. To have a prophecy fulfilled in their midst would have been stunning. The hometown boy, Jesus, had just declared Himself to be the Messiah. Jesus explains that He was the fulfillment of Isaiah's prophecy as it says, "The Spirit of the Lord is upon me, because he has anointed me to proclaim good news to the poor." Jesus was claiming to be God's chosen Messiah. Not only this, He was proclaiming that He would preach good news or the gospel to the poor, captives, blind, and oppressed. Jesus was sent to proclaim good news to those who were spiritually poor (Matthew 5:3), those who were captive to sin (John 8:31–38), those who were spiritually blind and in spiritual darkness (Matthew 13:13), and oppressed by sin (John 8:31–38). Jesus would then give two stories of how two Gentiles, the widow of Zarephath (1 Kings 17:8–24) and Naaman the Syrian (2 Kings 5), received God's grace and not the Jews. Both Naaman and Zarephath lived in a time of widespread unbelief. Jesus' message was that He was the Christ and was sent to preach good news to sinners and free them, but warned of the danger of religious Jews rejecting Him because they would not see themselves as blind, prisoners, poor, and oppressed. Thus, the people in the synagogue tried to kill Jesus for this message (Luke 4:24–30). They were examples of those who could not let John the Baptist's preaching sink down into their hearts. There were still remnants of self-righteousness left in their hearts.

Jesus would move on in His ministry and, in Matthew 4:17, it says, "From that time Jesus began to preach, saying, 'Repent, for the kingdom of heaven is at hand.'" The word *repent* is in the present tense, infinitive mood, and active voice, meaning Jesus was preaching repentance and continued to preach repentance wherever He went. If we combine John the Baptist's message with Jesus' message, we could see the good news of repentance that was preached by both men:

"You need to see yourselves as no better than the Gentile pagans, as outside God's blessing, as outside God's Covenant people

(Luke 3:3). You need to see yourselves as spiritually poor, prisoners of sin, spiritually blind, and oppressed by sin (Luke 4:18). You must elevate your sins and wickedness, confess them and repent of them (Luke 3:4–5). You must bring down low all spiritual pride, self-righteousness, and self-reliance (Luke 3:5). You must see that you are under God's wrath (Luke 3:7). You must bear fruits of repentance (Luke 3:8). You must see that if you do not repent, you will be cut down and cast into hell (Luke 3:9). You must bear fruits of repentance in your life (Luke 3:10–14). You must prepare your hearts to receive the Messiah because He will save you and bring you to heaven or judge you and cast you into the fires of hell (Luke 3:15–17, John 3:27–36). You should see that Jesus is the Anointed One or the Christ (Luke 4:18–19). You should repent and believe Jesus' message (Mark 1:15). You must repent and believe in Jesus for the forgiveness of sins and salvation (John 3:36, Matthew 4:17)."

Therefore, we see the message of repentance as a reoccurring theme in Jesus' ministry. Jesus emphasized repentance just as much as believing in Him for salvation. The verses below capture Jesus preaching repentance:

- Mark 1:14–15—Now, after John was arrested, Jesus came into Galilee proclaiming the gospel of God and saying, "The time is fulfilled, and the kingdom of God is at hand; **repent** and believe in the gospel."
- Matthew 4:17—From that time on Jesus began to preach, "**Repent**, for the kingdom of heaven has come near."
- Matthew 11:20–24—Then He began to denounce the cities where most of His mighty works had been done, because they did not **repent**. "Woe to you, Chorazin! Woe to you, Bethsaida! For if the mighty works done in you had been done in Tyre and Sidon, they would have **repented** long ago in sackcloth and ashes. But I tell you, it will be more bearable on the day of judgment for Tyre and Sidon

than for you. And you, Capernaum, will you be exalted to heaven? You will be brought down to Hades, For if the mighty works done in you had been done in Sodom, it would have remained until this day. But I tell you that it will be more tolerable on the day of judgment for the land of Sodom than for you."
- Matthew 12:41—The men of Nineveh will rise up at the judgment with this generation and condemn it, for they **repented** at the preaching of Jonah, and behold, something greater than Jonah is here.
- Luke 5:31–32—And Jesus answered them, "Those who are well have no need of a physician, but those who are sick. I have not come to call the righteous but sinners to **repentance**."
- Luke 10:13–15—"Woe to you, Chorazin! Woe to you, Bethsaida! For if the mighty works done in you had been done in Tyre and Sidon, they would have repented long ago, sitting in sackcloth and ashes. But it will be more bearable in the judgment for Tyre and Sidon than for you. And you, Capernaum, will you be exalted to heaven? You shall be brought down to Hades."
- Luke 13:3—No, I tell you; but unless you **repent**, you will all likewise perish.
- Luke 13:5—No, I tell you; but unless you **repent**, you will all likewise perish.
- Luke 15:7—Just so, I tell you, there will be more joy in heaven over one sinner who **repents** than over ninety-nine righteous persons who need no repentance.
- Luke 15:10—Just so, I tell you, there is joy before the angels of God over one sinner who **repents**.

This is all to say that repentance was a recurring gospel message that was proclaimed by Jesus throughout His ministry. No repentance in one's life was tied to perishing eternally (Luke

13:3, 5). No repentance in one's life received Christ's condemnation (Matthew 11:20–24). No repentance in one's life showed spiritual blindness (Luke 5:31–32). No repentance in one's life showed you did not belong to God (Luke 15:7, 10). Jesus warned the Pharisees of a damning self-righteousness where one had outward moralism while remaining unrepentant on the inside or in the heart (Matthew 23:25–28). The message of repentance didn't just stop with Christ's earthly ministry. After His resurrection, He said this to His disciples in Luke 24:46–47, "Thus it is written, that the Christ should suffer and on the third day rise from the dead, and that **repentance for the forgiveness of sins** should be proclaimed in his name to all nations, beginning from Jerusalem." In other words, Jesus was saying that repentance toward the Lord Jesus Christ should be heralded to all nations. The gospel message of turning from sin and turning to Christ for the forgiveness of sins would be proclaimed to all nations.

So, what would James have in mind with *"cleansing your hands"* and *"purifying your hearts"*? James would have undoubtedly thought of repentance away from sin (James 4:7), and a loving and submissive faith toward the Lord Jesus Christ (James 4:8). We can see how influenced James would have been through John the Baptist's ministry as well as the Lord's ministry which called for inward heart repentance and outward repentance away from sin and toward God. Once again, let's paraphrase James' command as we end this chapter:

Cleanse your hands, you sinners, and purify your hearts, you double-minded, by raising up every valley and bringing low every mountain. Flee the wrath of God. Repent and bring forth fruits of repentance for the Judge is standing at the door and is ready to cut down every tree that does not bear good fruit and throw it in the fire that burns with unquenchable fire. Repent! Turn from your sins and embrace Jesus Christ through faith.

Chapter 4

The Gospel Call for Repentant Faith: Godly Sorrow for Sin against God

James 4:9—*Be wretched and mourn and weep. Let your laughter be turned to mourning and your joy to gloom.*

In the previous chapter, we were able to understand one dimension of repentance which is a turning away from sin. James will now give us another aspect of repentance and saving faith and he will give four aorist imperatives to be *"wretched," "mourn," "weep,"* and *"turn"* laughter and joy to mourning and gloom. Repentance certainly involves a turning away from sin and a turning to God. Repentance also carries with it an intellectual and emotional component where a sinner will realize and understand that their sin is against an omnipotent, omniscient, righteous, just, and holy God. The start of repentance is when someone has an understanding that they've sinned against God and this understanding of sinning against God will cause the affections and emotions to react in sorrow, mourning, and lamentation. Thus, these commands from James capture the intellectual understanding and emotional and affectional components of a godly sorrow for sin against God.

The first aorist imperative verb that we see is a command to be *"wretched"* which comes from *talaipóreó* which means to "suffer hardship or distress," "endure severe hardship," "intensely afflict," or "leaving someone in a wretched and miserable condition." This word is used to describe the emotional condition that arises from inner or outer torment. We should know that it's not the physical outer torment that James is calling for or any sort of purposeful outward punishment where one would walk on hot coals, lash themselves with a whip, purposefully sleep in the cold, wear instruments that will inflict pain, or any of the like. James is calling for the sinner to be afflicted by seeing themselves as sinners (James 4:8), seeing themselves as enemies of God (James 4:4), seeing themselves double-minded (James 4:8), seeing themselves at war with God (James 4:4), seeing themselves as proud (James 4:6), and seeing their true identity as a condemned sinner before the Lord. As we learned earlier, the word repentance comes from *metanoia* which is a "change of mind." However, when there is a true change of mind, it is radical. It is the difference between up and down, darkness and light, right and left, black and white, right and wrong, moral and immoral, reality and fantasy. When there is true repentance, a person will realize they've been wrong about sin, wrong about God, wrong about salvation, wrong about their standing before God, wrong about their priorities, wrong about their worldview, and much more. When James is calling his audience to be "wretched," he is calling for them to be deeply afflicted intellectually and emotionally for their sin against God.

The second aorist imperative verb that we see is a command to "mourn" which comes from *pentheó* which means to "mourn," "lament," or "feel guilt." Properly, it means to "grieve as one who is grieving over a death or for a severe and painful loss." Figuratively, it is "grieving over a personal hope that dies." It is the mourning that is manifested with deep inner grief and is so severe that it overwhelms a person to the point that it cannot be hidden. In classical Greek, it was used most often to express a sorrow which was outwardly expressed in some way by tears or laments. It has been described that this mourning and grief bring an ache to the heart which will inevitably bring unrestrainable tears to the eyes. It is important to note that this type of mourning is over one's personal sin. People in pagan religions mourn over the death of a loved one so this would not even come close to capturing what James has in mind. Charles Spurgeon has said of this word, "Let a man once feel sin for half an hour, really feel its tortures, and I warrant you he would prefer to dwell in a pit of snakes than to live with his sins . . . If you can look on sin without sorrow then you have never looked on Christ." This mourning is the deep inner grief and brokenness over one's sin against God.

The third aorist imperative verb that we see is a command to *"weep"* which comes from *klaió* which means to "weep," "mourn," or "lament." Properly it is to "weep aloud, expressing uncontainable and audible grief." This word is tied to wailing, weeping, lamentation, and crying that springs from feeling utterly hopeless which is brought on by uncontainable emotional pain. This word is used after Peter denied the Lord three times and went out and wept bitterly (Matthew 26:75, Mark 14:72, Luke 22:62). Another form of this word is *klauthmos* and it carries the same meaning. Jesus uses this word to describe the weeping and wailing that occur in hell for the unredeemed and the damned (Matthew 8:12; 13:42, 50; 22:13; 24:51; 25:30; Luke 13:28). Hell is filled with loud crying, mourning, and wailing. The damned in hell are weeping and wailing over their eternal condition. There is no repentance in hell, only a hopeless sorrow. James is calling for his audience to recognize their sin before God and rightly respond with deep-afflicted mourning. Unlike those in hell, the audience James was writing to had time to see their sin, mourn over their sin, and turn to Christ in faith.

The fourth aorist imperative verb is a command to *"turn"* which comes from *metastrephó* which means to "turn" or "change," but it can also mean to "corrupt" or "pervert." The idea of this word is to transform into something of an opposite character, thus, causing it to be different or changed. James is using this word to call his audience to a state of mourning and gloom rather than laughter and joy. The idea is that the audience James was writing to had the wrong countenance on sin and right-standing before God and they need to completely change their countenance. In essence, James is calling them to see themselves as condemned sinners whereas they saw themselves as justified saints.

So, how would James understand this repentant godly sorrow over sin? Would James have recalled any teaching by the Lord that addressed a repentant godly sorrow for sin? James would certainly be familiar with the Sermon on the Mount. James would certainly be familiar with the Beatitudes or kingdom attitudes of those who had inherited eternal life. However, before we review the Beatitudes, let's see how James would be impacted by the Lord's teaching on sin. To understand sin is to understand why James is calling for affliction, mourning, wailing, and turning.

Sin and Its Punishment

Jesus preached much on the deadliness of sin. Sin was never to be taken lightly. Sin was a big deal in God's eyes. Sin is why Jesus needed to come into the world and bear the wrath of God. Therefore, having the right understanding of sin is critical. A weak understanding of sin leads to a weak understanding of the work of Christ. A weak understanding of sin leads to a weak understanding of the gospel. A weak understanding of sin leads to a weak understanding of man's hopelessness and helplessness. Therefore, when James is calling his listeners to be afflicted, mourn, and wail, he is presupposing that his audience should have the right understanding of sin and its consequences.

A definition of *sin* would be helpful and James and the apostle John could both contribute to a definition of *sin*. *Hamartía,* also known as *"sin,"* carries the meaning of "missing the mark" or "loss (forfeiture) because of not hitting the target." Also, 1 John 3:4 helps define *sin* by saying, "Everyone who makes a practice of sinning also practices lawlessness; sin is lawlessness." *Anomia* comes to the English as *lawlessness,* with *A* meaning "not" and *nomos* meaning "law." Thus, we can understand that *sin* is lawlessness or disobedience against God's law. John can help us further define *sin* where he says in 1 John 5:17, "All unrighteousness is sin." *Unrighteousness* comes to us from *adikia,* with *A* meaning "not" and *díke* meaning "justice" or, properly, "God's standards (justice)." Thus, we can understand *sin* being "anything that does not conform to God's standard of righteousness and justice." James gives us yet another definition of *sin* and says in James 4:17, "So whoever knows the right thing to do and fails to do it, for him it is sin." Here we can see that sin is not only what we do, but also what we don't do. Thus, a good definition of *sin* would be as follows: **Sin is breaking God's law by either not doing what God's law demands or doing what God's law prohibits by any thought (Matthew 5:28), word (Matthew 5:22), deed (Matthew 5:39), or intent (Matthew 6:1).**

To define *sin* is helpful, but to understand God's disposition toward sin will help us understand why James would be calling for affliction, mourning, and wailing. In fact, from Scripture, we can understand that God **hates** sin and those who practice it (Psalm 5:5). God **abhors** the bloodthirsty and sinful man (Psalm 5:6). God is **angry** with wicked sinners (Psalm 7:11). God is ready to **destroy** wicked and unrepentant sinners (Psalm 7:12–13). God **hates** the wicked who love violence and sin (Psalm 11:5). God considers sin as being in **warfare with Him** (James 4:4). God considers sin as an **abomination** (Proverbs 22:12). God considers sin as **evil** (Psalm 7:9). The Bible gives a clear description on what God thinks and feels about sin. God is not partial to sin.

God is not indifferent to sin. God doesn't think sin is a trivial matter. No, the God of the Bible has made it abundantly clear how He feels about sin. God hates sin. God abhors sin. God is angry with sin. God is ready to destroy the unrepentant sinners. God sees sin as warfare against Him. God sees sin as an abomination. God sees win as evil. God sees sin as wicked.

When we see how God has dealt with sin, we are able to gain an even greater understanding of God's disposition toward sin by the destruction and devastation that sin brings. The very first sin man committed was disobeying God and eating from the tree of the knowledge of good and evil which occurred in the Garden of Eden (Genesis 3). Man was promised that the day he ate of the fruit, he would surely die (Genesis 2:17). The repercussions of one sin were astronomical, which included woman being cursed (Genesis 3:16), man being cursed (Genesis 3:17–19), the earth being cursed (Genesis 3:17), death coming into the world (Romans 5:12, 1 Corinthians 15:22), sin being imputed to all mankind (Romans 5:12), man's relationship with God breaking and man dying spiritually (Genesis 3:22–24), and man earning the wages of both physical and spiritual death (Romans 6:23). We can see the seriousness of sin by how God dealt with the first sin. Sin is serious. There is nothing that sin doesn't corrupt. Man's sinfulness and enmity toward God is most fully demonstrated by man's desire to kill God which was accomplished and put on display when man demanded that Jesus be crucified and put to death (Matthew 27:22–26, Luke 23:21).

The helpless state of man's condition, or depravity, due to sin can be seen by understanding how sin keeps man in a state of degeneracy as it corrupts his entire being. In Jeremiah 13:23, it says, "Can the Ethiopian change his skin or the leopard his spots? Neither can you do good who are accustomed to doing evil." Psalm 7:14 says, "Behold, the wicked man conceives evil and is pregnant with mischief and gives birth to lies." Ecclesiastes 7:20 says of man's sinful depravity, "Surely there is not a righteous man on earth who does good and never sins." Simply put, man can do nothing within himself to change his sin problem as sin has corrupted his whole being, which includes body, soul, and spirit. The only thing that man does is continually give birth to sin and wickedness. As Jesus said in John 3:6, "That which is born of the flesh is flesh, and that which is born of the Spirit is spirit." Man's depravity of flesh and sin only produces more flesh and sin and cannot produce righteousness or spiritual life. In Psalm 51:5, David says this of his corrupted nature due to sin, "Behold, I was brought forth in iniquity, and in sin did my mother conceive me." Additionally, in Genesis 6:5, it says this regarding man's proclivity and ability to sin and man's inability to do good, "The LORD saw that the wickedness of man was great in the earth, and that every intention of the thoughts of his heart was only evil continually." Here we learn of the depth of sin in that, once we are conceived, we are passed on a sin nature and from the time of conception, we only commit sin and evil. Therefore, the depth of sin corrupts man upon conception and perpetually keeps him in this state of open rebellion and sinfulness against God.

Because God hates sin, He must deal with it according to who He is. Because God is an infinite (1 Timothy 1:17), loving (Psalm 136, 1 John 4:17), just (Genesis 18:25, Deuteronomy 32:4, Job 34:10, Jeremiah 17:10, Ezekiel 18:1–32), good (Psalm 25:8, Mark 10:18), faithful (Lamentations 3:22–23), omniscient (Psalm 147:5, Hebrews 4:13), immutable (James 1:17, Numbers 23:19), omnipresent (Jeremiah 23:23–24), and holy (Isaiah 44:6, 45:5), He must punish sin. To leave sin unpunished would violate His character. To leave sin unpunished would be unloving. To leave sin unpunished would be unjust. To leave sin unpunished would be bad. To leave sin unpunished would be unfaithful to God's character. To leave sin unpunished would be unholy. Therefore, God needs to punish sin.

The punishment of sin is hell. Hell is a place of God's full wrath and is a place of blackest darkness (Jude 13, Matthew

22:13), filled with furious and concentrated fire everywhere (Matthew 13:42), where there is weeping and anger against God for the unrepentant Christ-rejecting and Christ-neglecting sinners (Matthew 8:12), where they will spend all eternity paying for every sin they've ever committed with no hope of escape (Luke 16:26), only the expectation of excruciating torments to their body, soul, and spirit (Matthew 10:28) and an undying conscience that will haunt them day and night, forever and ever, with no reprieve (Luke 16:25). God will either punish one's sins by sending one to hell or He will have taken His wrath out and punished His own Son for the sake of one's sins who has come to the Lord Jesus Christ in repentance and faith. To understand sin is fundamental to understand what James is commanding of his unregenerate audience. Now that we have an understanding of sin and the punishment for sin, let's understand how Jesus' teaching on the Beatitudes would have impacted James' call to be afflicted, mourn, and wail (2).

Christ's Teaching on Spiritual Bankruptcy and Mourning over Sin

Matthew 5:3—*Blessed are the poor in spirit, for theirs is the kingdom of heaven*

When Jesus was giving His Sermon on the Mount, He started by giving the attitudes of those who were part of His kingdom. It is important to note that Jesus pronounces blessing for all those who exhibit these attitudes. The word *blessed* comes from *makarios* which means "happy," "blessed," or "to be envied." This word describes a believer in an enviable or fortunate position where they receive God's favor and grace. This is the kind of happiness that comes from receiving divine favor. John Macarthur has said of this word, "It is a divine pronouncement, the assured benefit of those who meet the conditions God requires. It is a state of existence to God in which a person is blessed from God's perspective even when he or she doesn't feel happy or is experiencing good fortune. This does not mean a conferral of blessing or an exhortation to live a life worthy of blessing; rather, it is an acknowledgement that the ones indicated are blessed. Negative feelings, absence of feelings, or adverse conditions cannot take away the blessedness of those who exist in such a relationship with God." Therefore, we can know that the Beatitudes are the attitudes of those who have been divinely blessed by the Lord.

The opposite of being blessed would be to be cursed. When Jesus denounced towns or the Pharisees, He would give them "woes." *Woe* is translated from *ouai* and this word can be said as "alas!" or "woe" and uttered in grief or denunciation. It is an *onomatopoeic word*, an imitation of the sound, which serves as an interjection expression or a cry of intense distress, displeasure, or horror. In the Septuagint, it can be a funeral lament, which is used eight times in this expression; it can mean a cry to get attention, which is used four times in this expression; or, it can mean an announcement of doom, which is used forty-one times in this expression. Therefore, let us note that those who are blessed by God will have kingdom attitudes and those who are cursed will not possess kingdom attitudes.

The first observation that we should make is the order of the first beatitude. When Jesus preached on the Beatitudes, He gave them in a very specific and sequential order. The first attitude was to be the attitude that would set into motion the rest of the Beatitudes. The first attitude was to be the catalyst that started a chain reaction. The first attitude was to be the very basic foundation and starting point of the Christian faith. To put it another way, one will never be spiritually rich until they are spiritually poor. One will never mourn over sin if he cannot see his spiritual bankruptcy. One will never be broken over sin and show obedient meekness unless there is spiritual brokenness. One will never hunger and thirst for righteousness if they remain satiated and pleased with their sinful condition. Everything starts with being poor in spirit.

Second, we should see that blessedness from the Savior comes from bankruptcy in spirit. The first attitude Jesus pronounces a blessing over is being *"poor in spirit."* The word *poor* is translated from *ptóchos* which means to "crouch, cringe or cower down and hide oneself for fear." It is a picture of a person reduced to total destitution who crouched in a corner begging as he held out one hand for alms and hid his face with the other hand because he was ashamed of being recognized. There are different words to describe being in poverty and the Lord used the word that pictured absolute poverty and destitution. *Ptóchos* does not simply refer to honest poverty and the struggle needed to make ends meet, it refers to abject poverty which literally has nothing and which is in imminent danger of real starvation. In fact, this word is used to describe Lazarus who was so poor that he was desiring to eat whatever fell from the rich man's table because he was so destitute. There are two words in Greek which are used to describe being poor. *Penēs* describes a man who had to work for a living while struggling. It is a word to describe the working man who is not rich but is not destitute either. Instead of *penēs*, Matthew chooses to write *ptóchos* which is the man who crouches, cowers, hides his face, and holds out his hand for help because he has absolutely nothing.

Please note that the Lord announces blessing over bankruptcy in spirit. This is not bankruptcy of wealth. This is not bankruptcy of good friends. This is the bankruptcy of the inner man. This is the bankruptcy of the inner man's spirit. This is bankruptcy of the inner man's spirit over sin. To commit one sin is to be rich in trespasses. To commit one sin is to be rich in wickedness. To commit one sin is to be rich in abomination against the Lord. To commit one sin is to be the wealthiest owner of what God hates. To commit one sin is to be at enmity with God. To commit one sin is to be the commander-in-chief of an army at enmity with God. To commit one sin is to be the crowd that cried out, "Crucify Him, crucify Him!" To pray one prayer out of selfish intent to be the chief of sinners. To compare your own righteousness against someone else's and not against the righteousness of God is self-righteousness worthy of eternal hell.

Christ's masterful Sermon on the Mount should have brought the listeners to such brokenness and poverty of spirit. They should have understood that the most religious leaders did not possess a righteousness that gave entrance into the kingdom of heaven (Matthew 5:20). They should have understood that anger against one's brother was enough to send one to hell (Matthew 5:21–22). They should have understood that lusting in one's heart was enough to send one to hell (Matthew 5:27–30). They should have understood that they did not love their enemies and were not perfect like the Heavenly Father (Matthew 5:43–48). They should have seen that they had wrong motives and intentions in giving (Matthew 6:1–4), wrong motives in prayer (Matthew 6:5–15), wrong motives in fasting (Matthew 6:16–18), wrong priorities with money and wealth (Matthew 6:19–24), and wrong priorities on what to seek (Matthew 6:25–34). One sin in any area of one's life was enough to cast one into hell. They were to be perfect as their Heavenly Father is perfect, and this should have brought a poverty of spirit. Christ's exposition of the spirit of the law should have gutted their self-righteousness and brought poverty of spirit.

To be poor in spirit is to say that you have no righteousness to offer God. To be poor in spirit is not to say that you have a little bit of something, but rather, that you have a whole lot of nothing. To be poor in spirit is to acknowledge that you're rich in sin and worthy of hell. To be poor in spirit is to acknowledge that you're rich in wickedness and worthy of judgment. There is not one denarius of righteousness. There is not one mite of righteousness. However, there are talents upon talents and denarii upon denarii of sin. To be poor in spirit is to beat your breast, turn your face away from heaven and say, "God be merciful to me the sinner." To be poor in spirit is to say what David said in Psalm 51:4, "Against you, you only, have I sinned and done what is evil in your sight." To be poor in spirit is to say what Peter said after the miraculous catching of fish in Luke 5:8 where he said, "Depart from me, for I am a sinful man, O Lord."

When Jesus is pronouncing blessing on the poor in spirit, he is announcing blessing on those who realize their spiritual bankruptcy before the Lord. John the Baptist would say that these are the ones who have filled every valley, or rather, elevated and confessed their sins before God and brought down every mountain and hill, or rather, rejected all spiritual accomplishments and pride before the Lord. These are the ones who are smitten and shattered by their sin against God. There is no righteousness of water baptism for the poor in spirit. There is no righteousness of confirmation for the poor in spirit. There is no righteousness of giving to the church for the poor in spirit. There is no righteousness of good works for the poor in spirit. There is no righteousness of being a prayer warrior for the poor in spirit. There is no righteousness of church attendance and membership for the poor in spirit. There is no righteousness of being a Sunday school teacher for the poor in spirit. Poverty of spirit does not mean having the right view of human sexuality, having the right view of marriage, taking communion, or any of the like. No! Being poor of spirit is to be brokenhearted over sinning against God and the realization that one stands with no righteousness to claim before God. Having an attitude of self-righteousness, self-importance, being a religious achiever, or having good morality is to be rich in spirit, but it is not the attitude of the poor in spirit. For the poor in spirit, there is simply a lowliness that is brought on by one's own sin and absolute spiritual destitution.

Oswald Chambers has said of this first beatitude, "As long as we have a conceited, self-righteous idea that we can do the thing if God will help us, God has to allow us to go on until we break the neck of our ignorance over some obstacle, then we will be willing to come and receive from Him. The bedrock of Jesus Christ's kingdom is poverty, not possession; not decisions for Jesus Christ, but a sense of absolute futility, 'I cannot begin to do it.' . . . The knowledge of our own poverty brings us to the moral frontier where Jesus Christ works." Martyn Lloyd-Jones has said this regarding being poor in spirit, "It means a complete absence of pride, a complete absence of self-assurance and of self-reliance. It means a consciousness that we are nothing in the presence of God. It is nothing, then, that we can produce; it is nothing that we can do in ourselves. It is just this tremendous awareness of our utter nothingness as we come face-to-face with God." J. C. Ryle has said this of poverty of spirit, "He means the humble, and lowly-minded, and self-abased; he means those who are deeply convinced of their own sinfulness in God's sight: these are people who are not 'wise in their own eyes and clever in their own sight' (Isaiah 5:21). They are not 'rich' and have not 'acquired wealth'; they do not fancy they 'do not need a thing'; they regard themselves as 'wretched, pitiful, poor, blind and naked' (Revelation 3:17). Blessed are all such! Humility is the very first letter in the alphabet of Christianity. We must begin low, if we want to build high."

Third, we should see that blessing is pronounced by the Lord on such people who have the right view of sin, who have the right view of their helpless depraved state, and who have the right view of the exalted holiness of God. Sinclair Ferguson has rightly said this about poverty of spirit, "There is much teaching on how to be filled with the Spirit, but where can we learn what it means to be spiritually emptied—emptied of self-confidence, self-importance, and self-righteousness? The sad truth is that we know so little of the blessing of which Christ speaks (and which He gives) because we are all too often full of ourselves and our own means of blessing. In fact, there is no sadder commentary on our lack of this spiritual poverty than the readiness so many of us have to let others know what we think. But the man who is poor in spirit is the man who has been silenced by God and seeks only to speak what he has learned in humility from Him." It is important to understand that poverty of spirit is an ongoing attitude and not just a one-time attitude. This is simply to say true believers don't escape or graduate past an attitude of being poor in spirit. Being smitten over sin and seeing oneself as helpless and dependent on the Lord is the absolute start of the Christian life.

There is not one milligram of grace from heaven that falls on those who are not poor in spirit. To not be poor in spirit is to receive no grace. To not be poor in spirit is to be outside the kingdom of heaven. To not be poor in spirit is to be under the prince of the power of the air. To not be poor in spirit is to be going through the broad gate and walking the broad path to destruction. However, for those that have seen their sin as God sees it, have seen the punishment that they rightly deserve, and declare their utter bankruptcy before God, they are those who become rich. Those who become poor in spirit, will become rich in God's kingdom. Those who have poverty in spirit become those who inherit every spiritual blessing as Paul says in Ephesians 1:3, "Blessed be the God and Father of our Lord Jesus Christ, who has **blessed us in Christ with every spiritual blessing** in the heavenly places." Those who are poor in spirit are in the kingdom of heaven. It means that those who are poor in spirit are in the kingdom of heaven over which God reigns. They are blessed because in the kingdom of heaven, they are rich in mercy, peace, joy, wisdom, love, joy, peace, and goodness. To be the subject of the eternal Lord, God, and King is where true happiness and blessedness spring from.

Christ frequently encountered this problem where followers could not acknowledge their spiritual poverty. When Christ gave a sermon in His hometown of Nazareth and declared that He was the Messiah who was sent to preach to the poor, the captives, the blind, and the oppressed and that God had bypassed the Jews and shown favor to two Gentiles in a time of widespread unbelief, the people in the synagogue were angry and wanted to kill Him (Luke 4:18–30). The religious crowd could not tolerate being told they were poor, captives, blind, and oppressed. In the same way, the Pharisees rejected John the Baptist's baptism for repentance because they saw themselves as righteous (Luke 7:30). Jesus told the Pharisees that He had come for the spiritually sick and not for the spiritually well (Luke 5:31–32). Jesus warned the Pharisees of justifying themselves before men and not seeing that God knew what was in the heart (Luke 16:15).

One of the most poignant examples of spiritual bankruptcy versus spiritual pride can be found in Luke 18 where Jesus gives a parable of a Pharisee and a tax collector. Jesus told this parable because there were some who trusted in their own righteousness while treating others with contempt (Luke 18:9). Both men went up to the temple to pray (Luke 18:10). Please note that both men went to a place where religious worship takes place. This was not a synagogue, rather, it was the Jewish temple. There could not have been a more religious place in all of Israel to go to pray. The Pharisee offered up a prayer to himself and said this in Luke 18:11, "God, I thank you that I am not like other men, extortioners, unjust, adulterers, or even like this tax collector." Please note that the Pharisee's prayer offered up his own righteousness. The Pharisee thanked God for his moral excellence. The Pharisee's standard of righteousness was compared to the righteousness of others and not to God. The Pharisee's righteousness was viewing what was on the outside and not on the inside. The Pharisee's righteousness was not one of looking inward on the heart. The Pharisee's righteousness was not from the heart but was simply that which is external. Notice in Luke 18:12 what the Pharisee says about his religious righteousness, "I fast twice a week; I give tithes of all that I get." There was no fasting that was required except on the Day of Atonement. This Pharisee thought he was religious and righteous by his excessive fasting. This Pharisee looked at his tithing and offering and was pleased within himself. Please note how blind this Pharisee was. This Pharisee couldn't even see that he was required to offer a burnt sacrifice for his sin. This Pharisee couldn't see that God should have treated him like the burnt offering and that he should be the one to die, have his throat cut, and be burned up in divine judgment. This Pharisee didn't need his ego stroked, he needed his pride crushed. John the Baptist would say that the Pharisee could not bring down the mountains of self-righteousness and bring up the valley of sins in the heart.

However, we see a tax collector who stood far off. The tax collector was seen as a traitor to Judaism where he would buy a tax franchise from the Roman government to collect taxes and pilfer additional taxes from his own people. He was seen as a traitor. He was seen as a sinner. He was seen as vile. This tax collector stood a long way off and could not even lift his eyes to heaven, but beat his breast and said this in Luke 18:13, "God, be merciful to me, the sinner." The tax collector could not bear to come close for worship. He had nothing to commend himself. He saw no righteousness in himself. He was one who was poor in spirit. He was one who cowered away with complete destitution. He did not have one milligram of righteousness to commend himself to God. Instead, he saw his sins and the obligation for a holy and righteous God to judge his sins. He saw that there was only judgment and wrath. Therefore, the tax collector cowered before God and asked for mercy, and not for justice. The tax collector asked for pardon and not punishment. Jesus would declare the tax collector righteous when he said this in Luke 18:14, "I tell you, this man went down to his house justified, rather than the other. For everyone who exalts himself will be humbled, but the one who humbles himself will be exalted." Poverty of spirit is the foundation of the Christian attitude. It is complete destitution and bankruptcy of spirit. For the tax collector in the parable, he didn't go back home without mercy. He didn't go home empty-handed. He didn't go home disappointed. No, he went home a pardoned sinner. He went back home declared righteous before the throne of God. He went back home exalted and rich with every spiritual, heavenly blessing for he humbled himself before God and God who is rich in mercy, tender-hearted, a friend of sinners, and an empathetic high priest made his scarlet sin as white as snow. Because he humbled himself before God, never ever would God remember his sins.

However, the Pharisee left the temple without pardon of sin, without entrance into the kingdom, and without true righteousness. Because the Pharisee exalted himself, God would not exalt him. The New Testament is filled with the record of people who could not see themselves as the spiritually bankrupt and who could not and would not humble themselves in light of their sin.

This is what James is calling for when he is commanding his unconverted listeners to be wretched. He is commanding them to see themselves as spiritual beggars. James is commanding them to be afflicted and broken over their spiritual condition. James is wisely calling for this necessary attitude of every Christian who enters the kingdom. This is the attitude of being afflicted for one's sin, broken for one's iniquity, troubled for one's trespasses, wretched for one's wickedness, miserable for one's maliciousness, and distressed for one's blasphemy. Christ called for this first beatitude of poverty of spirit as it is the foundation of where one needs to start. James is following Christ's example and calling for poverty of spirit.

Matthew 5:4—*Blessed are those who mourn, for they shall be comforted*

As we noted above, poverty of spirit is the foundation of the Christian faith. Every believer that enters into the kingdom of God enters as spiritually destitute. Every believer that enters into the kingdom of God enters with no religious achievement, no boasting of morality, no self-reliance, no self-righteousness, and no pride. The believer that enters the kingdom of God beats his breast, he doesn't stroke his ego. The believer that enters the kingdom of God cries for mercy, not for justice. The first beatitude sets in motion the rest of the Beatitudes. This is most certainly what James had in mind when he called his unconverted listeners to be afflicted. His next set of commands was to be wretched, mourn, wail, and let one's laughter be turned to mourning and joy to gloom. This is where we'll see how James was influenced by Christ's teaching on the second beatitude.

This attitude of mourning is a far cry from what the world promotes. The world promotes happiness and fulfillment. The world promotes the pursuit of a good career. The world promotes finding the ideal spouse. The world promotes buying and building the perfect house. The world promotes self-improvement. The world promotes self-esteem. The world does not promote mourning over sin, but especially not mourning over one's own sin against a just and holy God. To see oneself as spiritually bankrupt, destitute, deserving of eternal hell, and mourning over this condition is completely antithetical to the world's system. However, this attitude is right in line with someone in Christ's kingdom.

First, let's note that the words *weep, mourn,* and *wail* carry the idea of deep inner grief that leads to outward lamentation and sorrow. To follow the Beatitudes sequentially, we see that this mourning comes from one's spiritual bankrupt condition over sin. This mourning is not over earthly or worldly things such as losing a job, losing a loved one, being materially poor, or any of the like. This mourning is strictly related to the mourning over one's sin and spiritual bankruptcy.

Second, let's see that the verb *mourning* is in the present tense. In other words, this attitude is not something that a Christian will graduate from. It is not to say that a true Christian is always weeping and mourning externally. However, it is to say that the true Christian is continually aware of their spiritual bankruptcy, capacity to sin, and the negative influence of sin in one's life and this causes mourning. A. W. Pink has said this of mourning over sin, "This 'mourning' is by no means to be confined unto the initial experience of conviction and contrition, for observe the tense of the verb: it is not 'have mourned,' but 'mourn'—a present and continuous experience. The Christian himself has much to mourn over. The sins which he now commits—both of omission and commission—are a sense of daily grief to him, or should be, and will be, if his conscience is kept tender. An ever-deepening discovery of the depravity of his nature, the plague of his heart, the sea of corruption within—ever polluting all that he does—deeply exercises him. Consciousness of the surgings of unbelief, the swellings of pride, the coldness of his love, and his paucity of fruit, make him cry, 'O wretched man that I am.'"

Joel 2:12–13 captures a mourning and contrition of the heart where the LORD says, "'Yet even now,' declares the LORD, 'return to me with all your heart, with fasting, with weeping, and with mourning; and rend your hearts and not your garments.' Return to the LORD your God, for he is gracious and merciful, slow to anger, and abounding in steadfast love; and he relents over disaster." John Macarthur has rightly said that the hindrances to mourning over sin are hardness of heart, resisting the Holy Spirit, and a heart of stone which can be brought on by a love of sin, despair, conceit, presumption, procrastination, and shallowness.

So, what is there to mourn over? What sin is there that could possibly keep a Christian in a present tense state of mourning? James alone highlights several areas of sin that a Christian could mourn over. A Christian could see they are slow to rejoice over trials (James 1:2), that they lack perseverance in trials (James 1:3), that they don't seek God for wisdom (James 1:5), that they doubt God (James 1:6), that they are easily tempted and dragged into sin (James 1:14–15), that they are quick to become angry (James 1:19–20), that they hear the Word of God but don't practice it (James 1:22), that they don't control their tongue (James 1:26, 3:1–12), that they show favoritism (James 2:1–9), that they stumble in many ways (James 3:2), that they may become bitter and selfish (James 3:14). James gave a warning in his epistle on the seriousness of sin and being a lawbreaker where he says in James 2:10, "For whoever keeps the whole law but fails in one point has become guilty of all of it." In other words, just one sinful intent, one sinful thought, one sinful action, one sinful act of omission puts one in the category of being a lawbreaker and in the realm of divine judgment. James knew the requirements of the law and the consequences that it brought. To James, sin was serious and one sin was serious enough to render one guilty of breaking the entire law and to be under God's judgment. Such an understanding of sin by the Christian will lead to continuous mourning over sin. Even when the Christian is redeemed, regenerated, converted, and saved, they will mourn over the very sins they commit which put their Lord on the cross. Although the believer is pardoned from all sins when they are justified, there is still a mourning over sins as the believer will inevitably do the very things that God hates which is sin. Such a mourning over sin by the believer is evidence of divine blessing.

James would know of the seriousness of sin and heard Jesus preach on sin. Jesus would say that one could mourn over adulterous and lustful thoughts (Matthew 5:27–28), mourn over not keeping your word (Matthew 5:33–37), mourn over not loving one's enemies (Matthew 5:43–47), mourn over falling short of God's perfect righteousness (Matthew 5:48), mourn over worldliness and loving wealth (Matthew 5:19–24), mourn over being anxious and not trusting God (Matthew 5:25–34), mourn over hypocritical judging (Matthew 7:1–6), mourn over our lack of zeal for the lost (Matthew 9:35–38), mourn over our resiliency to trust Christ in everything (Matthew 14:31), mourn over our hastiness to pronounce judgment on others (Luke 9:54), mourn over the desire for greatness (Matthew 18:1–6), mourn over being slow to forgive (Matthew 18:21–35). There are many things that a Christian can mourn over and should continue to mourn over. Sin should never be trivialized. Jesus Christ hung on the cross naked and suffered the wrath of God on the cross for sin. Only the damned in hell will have an idea of what Christ suffered on the cross. There is no shortage of sin in one's life that should prevent a Christian from mourning. Paul saw this very sin in his own life as he evaluated his own life and saw his continual sin on a minute by minute and second by second basis where he says in Romans 7:24, "Wretched man that I am! Who will deliver me from this body of death?" Although he had been born again, converted, and saved with a new heart, new mind, new affections, and new will, he still saw sin in his life, and this caused him deep grief.

There are examples where true believers felt the pain of their sin. For example, Jesus had prophesied that Peter would betray Him three times before the rooster crowed. Peter was a true believer in Christ (John 13:9–10) and Jesus had prayed that Peter's faith would not fail and that Peter would be strengthened by the trial that was to come (Luke 22:31). However, Peter would deny Christ three times and claimed no allegiance with Christ. When Peter denied Jesus the third time, the Lord turned and looked at Peter and Peter went out and wept bitterly (Luke 22:61–62). Peter would have certainly remembered the words of Jesus when He sent out His disciples and said this in Matthew 10:32–33, "So everyone who acknowledges me before men, I also will acknowledge before my Father who is in heaven, but whoever denies me before men, I also will deny before my Father who is in heaven." Peter had just denied the Lord before men. Peter had just denied the Lord before women which would be even less intimidating than men. Peter had just denied the Lord and he would have surely remembered this promise, "Whoever denies me before men, I also will deny before my Father who is in heaven." This was sin of the greatest magnitude. This was sin that denied Christ but would not deny himself. This was sin that would not take up a cross and confess Christ. This was being ashamed of Christ (Luke 9:26). Peter's response was appropriate where he went out and wept bitterly for denying Christ, being ashamed of Christ, and not acknowledging Christ. This is being heartbroken, rending one's heart, and mourning for sin against God.

This is one example of how believers are to think about their sin and mourning for their sin. When is the last time you ever mourned over your sin? Have you ever mourned over your sin? For those who have never mourned over sin against God, you should question whether you've been truly born again. Have you been afraid to proclaim Christ publicly? Have you lacked zeal in reaching the lost for Christ? Have you compared your righteousness to others like a Pharisee? Have you preached a false gospel? Have you been short-tempered? Have you neglected helping someone in need? Have you performed religious activity for the sake of being recognized? Have you hidden your sin rather than confessed it? Have you superficially looked at sin like a Pharisee? Have you neglected looking at the sins in your own heart? Such sin should cause a stiff neck to break and the heart to be rent. Such sin should cause the breast to be beat and the face to be downcast. This is the sin that put Christ on the cross. Think about the price that Christ paid for sin. Jesus needed to be rejected by God (Isaiah 53:3), so we could be resurrected by God (1 Corinthians 15:52). Jesus needed to be despised (Isaiah 53:3), so we would not be damned (Romans 1:18–32). Jesus needed to be crushed by God (Isaiah 53:5, 10), so we would not be cursed by God (Galatians 3:13). Jesus needed to be crucified (Isaiah 53:5), so we could be justified (Romans 3:24). Jesus needed to be forsaken (Matthew 27:46), so we could be forgiven (Isaiah 53:12). Jesus suffered (Isaiah 53:11), so we would be saved (Matthew 1:23). Jesus needed to suffer the wrath of God (Isaiah 53:10), so He could show forth the riches of God (Ephesians 2:7). Jesus needed to be resurrected (Isaiah 53:11), so we could be perfected (Hebrews 10:14). Jesus needed to bear reproach (Hebrews 13:13), so we could be redeemed (Romans 3:24). Jesus offered himself as a sacrifice (Hebrews 9:26), so we could be saints (2 Corinthians 5:21). One who has not and is not mourning over sin demonstrates they possess a hard heart (Luke 8:12), an unrepentant heart (Luke 13:3, 5), an uncircumcised heart (Deuteronomy 10:16), and a proud and self-exalted heart (Luke 18:14).

In Luke's account of the Beatitudes, we can gain an even greater understanding of the disaster when one cannot see themselves as spiritually poor and mourn over their sins where Jesus says this in Luke 6:24, "But woe to you who are rich, for you have received your consolation. Woe to you who are full now, for you shall be hungry. Woe to you who laugh now, for you shall mourn and weep." Just as Jesus pronounces blessing on those who are poor in spirit and mourn over sin, He likewise pronounces curses on those who will not see themselves spiritually bankrupt and mourn over sin. Therefore, we can clearly see that those who are not poor in spirit have the wrong view of sin, wrong view of themselves, wrong view on the seriousness of sin, wrong view of the cross, wrong view of Jesus Christ, and more. To not be poor in spirit and mourning over sin is to completely misunderstand the definition of *sin,* the depth of sin, the death that sin brings, the destruction of sin, the devastation of sin, and the punishment of sin. To not be poor in spirit and mourning over sin is to completely misunderstand Jesus' teaching on sin and Jesus' substitutionary atonement for sin on the cross.

Third, note that those who are mourning over their sin will be comforted. The word *comforted* comes from *parakaleó* which can mean "comfort," "encourage," or "console." Those who are mourning over their sin will be comforted by the Holy Spirit (John 14:16). Those who are mourning over sin will be assured by the Holy Spirit that they are children of God (Romans 8:15–16).

Those who mourn will know that they have the right relationship with the Father through Jesus Christ (Romans 5:1), that they've been forgiven (Romans 4:6), that they have inherited eternal life (John 17:3), that Christ has dealt with their iniquity on the cross (John 19:30), that Christ will take them to be with the Father (John 14:1–3), that nothing will separate them from the love of God that is in Christ Jesus (John 6:37–40, 10:28–29). This is the comfort that those who are bankrupt in spirit and are mourning over sin will receive. Martyn Lloyd-Jones has this to say about this second beatitude:

"Let us then try to define this man who mourns. What sort of man is he? He is a sorrowful man, but he is not morose. He is a sorrowful man, but he is not a miserable man. He is a serious man but he is not a solemn man. He is a sober-minded man but he is not a sullen man. He is a grave man but he is never cold. There is with his gravity, a warmth and an attraction. This man is serious, but because of these views which he has, and his understanding of truth, he also has 'a joy unspeakable and full of glory.' So he is like the apostle Paul, 'groaning within himself,' and yet happy because of his experience of Christ and the glory that is to come. The Christian is not superficial in any sense, but is fundamentally serious and fundamentally happy. You see, the joy of the Christian is a holy joy, the happiness of the Christian is a serious happiness. None of that superficial appearance of happiness and joy! No, no; it is a solemn joy, it is a holy joy, it is a serious happiness; so that, though he is grave and sober-minded and serious, he is never cold and prohibitive. Indeed, he is like our Lord Himself, groaning, weeping, and yet, 'for the joy that was set before him' enduring the cross, despising the shame. That is the man who mourns; that is the Christian. That is the type of Christian seen in the Church in ages past, when the doctrine of sin was preached and emphasized, and men were not merely urged to take a sudden decision. A deep doctrine of sin, a high doctrine of joy, and the two together produce this blessed, happy man who mourns, and who at the same time is comforted."

As we close this section, we can see why James gives four commands to be afflicted, mourn, wail, and to turn one's affections the other direction. Those who remained unregenerate and unconverted were in need of a deep plowing of the heart. Those who remained unregenerate needed to raise up the valleys and confess and renounce sin. They needed to bring down their spiritual pride, self-righteousness, pride, and self-will. They needed to gain the right understanding of sin, the right understanding of judgment, and the right understanding of the attributes of God. Let us see that brokenness accompanies blessedness. Let us see that poverty of spirit produces prosperity in Christ. Once again, let's paraphrase James' commands to be afflicted, to mourn, and to wail as we end this chapter:

"Be afflicted, mourn, and wail over your sin. Rend your heart and not your garments. Woe to you who are rich in spirit and in need of nothing! Woe to you who laugh now and will not acknowledge your spiritual bankruptcy! Let your laughter be turned to mourning and your joy to gloom for whoever fails in keeping the law is guilty of breaking it all. Whoever is guilty of breaking the law at one point is liable to be thrown into hell which is a place of God's full wrath and is a place of blackest darkness, filled with furious and concentrated fire everywhere, where there is weeping and anger against God for the unrepentant Christ-rejecting and Christ-neglecting sinners, where they will spend all eternity paying for every sin they've ever committed with no hope of escape and only the expectation of excruciating torments to their body, soul, and spirit and an undying conscience that will haunt them day and night, forever and ever, with no reprieve. Therefore, be wretched, mourn, and wail, you sinners and you double-minded."

Chapter 5

The Gospel Call for a Humble Faith toward the Lord Jesus Christ

James 4:10—*"Humble yourselves before the Lord, and he will exalt you."*

This final aorist command is a summation of the previous nine commands and describes the truly humble person. The final aorist imperative that James gives to his audience is to *"humble yourselves."* The word *humble* comes from *tapeinoó* which means "to make low" or "to humble." This is to show true humility and true lowliness which happens by being fully dependent on the Lord. It is the humility that dismisses reliance upon self, such as one who practices self-government or self-will. It is the emptying of the carnal ego. This type of humility exalts the Lord as one's all-in-all and prompts the gift of His fullness in the believer. It is to be humble in the heart and it is to be abased or brought low.

James is commanding his listeners to voluntary submission and to be made low willingly. The idea of this word is that it is calling listeners to allow themselves to be humbled or placed under God. David Edmond Hiebert makes this comment about being humbled, "It is not to be a forced humiliation, but a voluntary self-abasement." John Macarthur makes this comment about the call for humbling oneself before God, "To make oneself low, not in the self-put-downs that many people use to induce others to build them up, but in a genuine realization of complete unworthiness and lostness because of sin. As the penitent sinner submits to God and draws closer to Him, like Isaiah he cries out, 'Woe is me, for I am ruined! Because I am a man of unclean lips, and I live among a people of unclean lips; for my eyes have seen the King, the Lord of hosts' (Isaiah 6:5). The more an unbeliever sees God as He really is, glorious and holy, the more clearly he sees himself as he really is, sinful and depraved." Therefore, humility is simply one coming to a biblical view of sin, self, the Savior, and salvation.

First, let's note that to humble oneself before the Lord is to look at the biblical bad news of sin, death, and hell. The bad news is that man has sinned, which is breaking God's law by either not doing what His law demands or doing what His law prohibits by any thought, word, deed, or intent. God's disposition toward sin is one of hatred, anger, abhorrence, defilement, wickedness, evil, hostility, and is warfare against Him. Man is incapable of curing his problem with sin. Man cannot propitiate the righteous anger of God, redeem himself, earn forgiveness, or be made right with God on his own merits. God's attributes such as being eternal, loving, just, good, faithful, omniscient, and immutable demand that God must punish sin. The punishment of sin is hell, which is a place of God's full wrath and a place of blackest darkness, filled with furious and concentrated fire everywhere, where there is weeping and anger against God for the unrepentant Christ-rejecting and Christ-neglecting sinners, where they will spend all eternity paying for every sin they've ever committed with no hope of escape and only the expectation of excruciating torments to their body, soul, and spirit and an undying conscience that will haunt them day and night, forever and ever, with no reprieve. True humility starts with a biblical view of sin and its consequences.

Second, note that to humble oneself before the Lord is to have the biblical view of the person of the Lord Jesus Christ. Jesus is the Jewish Messiah and Son of the Living God (Matthew 16:16). Jesus is God and He is coequal and coeternal with God the Father and God the Holy Spirit (John 5:17–18; 10:30, 38; 14:10). Jesus is the eternal, Only Begotten, one-of-a-kind, Son of God (John 3:16). Jesus is the Anointed One of God (Luke 4:18–19). Jesus is the Savior of the world (Luke 2:11). Jesus is the Creator and Sustainer of the Universe (John 1:1–14). Jesus is the Son of David (Matthew 1:1–16, Luke 3:23–38). Jesus was born of a virgin (Matthew 1:23). Jesus was the Word made flesh (John 1:14). Jesus was physically born into this world as a man (Matthew 1:25). Jesus is, thus, truly God and truly man. True humility understands and embraces the person of the Lord Jesus Christ.

Third, note that to humble oneself before the Lord is to have the biblical view of the work of the Lord Jesus Christ. The biblical view of Jesus' work is that Jesus lived a sinless life (Matthew 26:59–60) and fulfilled all righteousness found in the law and the prophets (Luke 24:44–46) and declared Himself to be the Christ (Matthew 16:16), the Only Begotten Son of the Living God through His teaching (John 3:16, Matthew 22:41–46), which was attested to by His miracles (John 10:37–38). Jesus offered himself as a spotless and blameless sacrifice for sin (John 1:29) to propitiate the righteous anger of God by taking all the sins of God's people (John 10:11) and, thus, the full wrath of God that was due to man (Matthew 26:39, 27:45–46; Luke 22:44). His sacrifice propitiated the righteous anger of God and reconciled and brought peace from man to God and God to man (Matthew 27:51, John 19:30). His substitutionary sacrifice and death also redeemed sinful man to Holy God by forgiving man's sin and imputing Christ's righteousness to man (1 Corinthians 5:21). Jesus was resurrected from the dead on the third day by His own power (John 10:18), by God the Father (Galatians 1:1) and God the Holy Spirit (Romans 8:11), which affirmed His person, His teachings, and salvific work for sinners (Romans 4:25). He ascended to the right hand of the Father (Luke 24:51) and is empowered with all authority to bring about the plan of salvation for all His people (Matthew 28:18) by causing them to be born again (John 3:1–10) and justified by His grace (John 3:16, 18, 36). He will also return to bring all His own to heaven with Him (John 6:37–40, 14:1–3) to be glorified (John 17:24) while also judging and condemning Satan, demons, and sinful man (Matthew 25:31–46, Revelation 20:7–15). True humility understands and embraces the work of the Lord Jesus Christ.

Fourth, note that to humble oneself before the Lord is to come to the Lord Jesus Christ according to His terms. Christ's terms to enter His kingdom are to repent and put one's faith in Him. *Repentance* is a gift from God where the sinner understands his sin against God and is poor in spirit (intellect), has godly sorrow and mourns over his sin against God (emotions and affections), and turns away from his sin and toward God for righteousness (will or volition). *Saving faith* is a gift from God where a sinner has knowledge of Jesus' person and work where a sinner will respond to Christ's person and work by denying themselves, picking up their cross, and lovingly and obediently submitting and committing their life to Jesus and trusting in Him only for salvation. True humility understands and accepts the Lord's terms to salvation.

Fifth, we should see that whoever is humble before the Lord will be exalted. This is to say that the Lord will bless the humbled sinner by seating him with Him in the heavenlies with every spiritual blessing (Ephesians 1:3). The humbled sinner is regenerated or born again by the Holy Spirit (John 3:1–10; 1 John 3:1; 1 Peter 1:3, 23; Titus 3:5; Ezekiel 11:19–20, 36:24–27; Jeremiah 24:7, 31:33–34, 32:38–40; Matthew 5:8). The humbled sinner is forgiven all his past, present, and future sins (Psalm 103:12, Isaiah 1:18, Ephesians 1:7, John 1:29, Micah 7:19, Romans 8:33–34, Hebrews 8:12). The humbled sinner is reconciled to God through Christ (2 Corinthians 5:19, Romans 5:10–11, Colossians 1:21–22). The humbled sinner becomes a child of God (Romans 8:16, Matthew 5:9). The humbled sinner possesses a right standing with God or justification before God (Romans 3:22–28). The humbled sinner is adopted into the family of God (Ephesians 1:5). The humbled sinner is raised up with Christ and seated in the heavenly realms (Ephesians 2:6). The humbled sinner is made a coheir with Christ (Romans 8:17). The humbled sinner receives Christ as their Great High Priest (Hebrews 4:14). The humbled sinner receives God as their Heavenly Father (Romans 8:15). The humbled sinner receives Christ as their brother (Hebrews 2:11–12). The humbled sinner receives eternal life (John 17:3). The humbled sinner receives the Holy Spirit (Galatians 3:2, 14; Ephesians 1:13; 1 Corinthians 12:13; 2 Corinthians 1:21–22). The humbled sinner's salvation is eternally secure (John 6:37–40, 10:28–29, 17:1–26; Romans 8:31–38). The humbled sinner's sins were all punished in Christ on the cross (2 Corinthians 5:21; Romans 3:25, 5:19; Galatians 3:13, 2:20; John 10:11, 19:30; Hebrews 9:25–29, Colossians 2:13–15; Isaiah 53:1–12). The humbled sinner has the guarantee that Christ will bring them to be with Him forever in heaven (John 14:1–3, 17:24; Hebrews 11:6; Revelation 21:1–7, 22:1–5). The humbled sinner will reign forever with God (Revelation 22:5). The humbled sinner will not be touched by the second death (Revelation 2:11). The humbled sinner will have a resurrected and glorified body (1 Corinthians 15:12–58). The humbled sinner now has the mind of Christ (1 Corinthians 2:16). The humbled sinner inherits the kingdom of heaven (Matthew 5:3). The humbled sinner is comforted by God (Matthew 5:4). The humbled sinner inherits everything the Father possesses (Matthew 5:5). The humbled sinner is filled with righteousness (Matthew 5:6). The humbled sinner is given mercy and pardon for sin (Matthew 5:7). The humbled sinner will receive a joyful welcome into Christ's kingdom (Matthew 25:21). The humbled sinner will be rewarded by the Lord Jesus Christ (Matthew 25:23). The humbled sinner has confidence before God in judgment (Matthew 25:31–40). The humbled sinner will worship God in spirit and in truth (John 4:24). The humbled sinner will worship the Lord in heaven for all eternity (Revelation 7:9–17). The humbled sinner is part of the Bride of Christ (Revelation 22:17). So, what does it mean that the Lord will exalt one who humbles himself before Him? It is to say that the Lord Jesus Christ will save this person and bless them with every spiritual blessing (Ephesians 1:3, Matthew 25:34).

We see that James ends his exhortation with a command to humble oneself before the Lord. We can clearly see how influenced James was by the teaching and preaching of the Lord as James gives these ten aorist imperatives to come to the Lord in saving faith. James was calling for a submissive, self-denying, cross-bearing, preeminent loving, repentant, and humble faith in the Lord Jesus Christ. If we were to put together the gospel call of James, it could be stated this way from what we have developed thus far:

"Woe to you who are rich in spirit and in need of nothing! Woe to you who laugh now and will not acknowledge your spiritual bankruptcy! Be afflicted, weep, mourn, and wail over your sin. Rend your heart and not your garments. Let your laughter be turned to mourning and your joy to gloom for whoever fails in keeping the law is guilty of breaking it all. Whoever is guilty of breaking the law at one point is liable to be thrown into hell which is a place of God's full wrath and is a place of blackest darkness, filled with furious and concentrated fire everywhere, where there is weeping and anger against God for the unrepentant Christ-rejecting and Christ-neglecting sinners, where they will spend all eternity paying for every sin they've ever committed with no hope of escape and only the expectation of excruciating torments to their body, soul, and spirit and an undying

conscience that will haunt them day and night, forever and ever, with no reprieve. Cleanse your hands, you sinners, and purify your hearts, you double-minded, by raising up every valley and bringing low every mountain. Flee the wrath of God that is coming. Repent and bring forth fruits of repentance for the Judge is standing at the door and is ready to cut down every tree that does not bear good fruit and throw it in the fire that burns with unquenchable fire. Repent! Turn from your sins and toward the Lord Jesus Christ. Submit therefore to God by denying yourself and take your stand against the devil. Hate your father and mother and wife and children and brothers and sisters, yes, and even your own life. Renounce all that you have. Draw near to God and He will draw near to you. Draw near to God with your heart by loving the Lord Jesus Christ with all your heart, and with all your soul, and with all your mind, and with all your strength. Take up your cross and follow the Lord Jesus Christ. Humble yourself before the Lord and He will exalt you and give you the free gift of eternal life that you may have fellowship with the Father. For what would it profit yourself if you gained the whole world and forfeited your soul? Or what could you give in exchange for your soul?"

Nicodemus: The Ritualistic, Legalistic, Ceremonial, Exalted Jewish Pharisee Becomes the Redeemed, Loyal, Cross-Bearing, Humble Jesus Follower

John 3:1—*Now there was a man of the Pharisees named Nicodemus, a ruler of the Jews.*

John 19:38–40—*After these things Joseph of Arimathea, who was a disciple of Jesus, but secretly for fear of the Jews, asked Pilate that he might take away the body of Jesus, and Pilate gave him permission. So he came and took away his body. Nicodemus also, who earlier had come to Jesus by night, came bringing a mixture of myrrh and aloes, about seventy-five pounds in weight. So they took the body of Jesus and bound it in linen cloths with the spices, as is the burial custom of the Jews.*

To illustrate humbling oneself before the Lord, it would be most beneficial to see how the Lord worked this out in the life of Nicodemus who was a Pharisee. We will compare Nicodemus' life to that of his pharisaical peers. We will inevitably see two paths. One path is that of a pharisaical, false-teaching, religious Jewish leader who is brought to salvation. The other path is one where pharisaical, false-teaching, religious Jewish leaders will not humble themselves and the wrath of God remains on them. We will follow Nicodemus' story in the Bible and draw inferences from Jesus' interactions with the Pharisees to demonstrate Nicodemus' ongoing knowledge of the person and works of the Lord Jesus Christ. We will start with Jesus teaching Nicodemus on the New Birth or Regeneration.

The Teacher of Israel Humbled by Jesus' Teaching on Regeneration and Salvation

John 3:1—*Now there was a man of the Pharisees named Nicodemus, a ruler of the Jews.*

Pharisees were the religious teachers during the time of Christ. At the time of Christ, Josephus records that there were about 6,000 Pharisees in Israel. The term *Pharisee* comes from the term "separated." Pharisees are depicted in a very negative light in the New Testament, but during this specific time in Israel, they were seen as the conservative religious leaders. They were zealous to keep the law and they were the experts on Scripture. Pharisees were meticulous about preserving both the Old Testament Scripture as well as oral tradition. Nicodemus was not only a Pharisee, he was also a member of the Jewish Sanhedrin. There were two classes of Jewish courts which were called *Sanhedrin*. There was the Great Sanhedrin and the Lesser Sanhedrin. A Lesser Sanhedrin of twenty-three judges was appointed to sit as a tribunal in each city, but there was only supposed to be one

Great Sanhedrin of seventy-one judges which, among other roles, acted as the Supreme Court. The Great Sanhedrin would take appeals from cases which were passed to them by lesser courts. To put it in modern terms, there were state Supreme Courts and Federal Supreme Courts, and Nicodemus was a member of the Federal Supreme Court. There were seventy-one judges on the Great Sanhedrin in the case of an even vote so that the seventy-first member could be the tiebreaker. In the modern American era, judges that are on the Supreme Court have not only attended the best law schools, they have also served on smaller circuits, gained experience, and are considered experts in the law. In the same way, Pharisees were experts in Old Testament Scripture and the law. They were knowledgeable in Scripture and were considered the premier teachers in Israel.

Nicodemus would have also had an upbringing that was strong in preserving and teaching Judaism. Jewish women were very important in the life of the child. If Jewish women were faithful to their religion, they would know of many of the noble Hebrew mothers and would seek to follow their example. The children would be trained from infancy to recognize God as their Father and as Maker of the world. They were trained to have knowledge of the laws from earliest youth and to have these impressed in their souls or, rather, engraven on their souls. This would have been a command from Deuteronomy 6:6–7, "And these words that I command you today shall be on your heart. You shall teach them diligently to your children, and shall talk of them when you sit in your house, and when you walk by the way, and when you lie down, and when you rise," and Deuteronomy 11:18–19, "You shall therefore lay up these words of mine in your heart and in your soul, and you shall bind them as a sign on your hand, and they shall be as frontlets between your eyes. You shall teach them to your children, talking of them when you are sitting in your house, and when you are walking by the way, and when you lie down, and when you rise." The children were brought up learning, exercised in the laws, and made acquainted with the acts of their predecessors to imitate them.

However, while the earliest religious teaching would, of necessity, come from the mother, it was the father who was "bound to teach his son." He was to impart to his child the knowledge of the Torah with great spiritual clarity as if he had been the one to receive the law from Mount Horeb. Every engagement was to be a time where he could teach his child, even at the necessary mealtime. The men were to see this as serious labor that would not prove fruitless. In fact, men who had sons and had failed to bring them up in the knowledge of the law were considered profane and vulgar. Therefore, the man had a high duty and calling to instruct his child.

When the child learned to speak, his religious instruction was to begin. Such instruction would begin with verses from Scripture which could include Jewish liturgy, such as the Shema, which would have certainly included Deuteronomy 6:4–5, "Hear, O Israel: The LORD our God, the LORD is one. You shall love the LORD your God with all your heart and with all your soul and with all your might." There was special attention given to memory since forgetfulness might prove fatal in its consequences as this might lead to ignorance or neglect of the law.

Very early, the child would be taught what might be called his *birthday text*, which was some verse of Scripture beginning with, ending with, or at least containing the same letters as his Hebrew name. This verse would be inserted in the child's daily prayers. There were also hymns they were taught which would be the Psalms for the days of the week, or festive Psalms, such as the Hallel (Psalms 113–118).

Regular instruction would begin when the child reached the age of five or six years (according to strength). This is when the child would be sent to school. There are several references to schools existing throughout the land and almost every period. The existence of higher schools and academies would not have been possible without a primary education. Tradition ascribes to Joshua the son of Gamla the introduction of schools in every town and the compulsory education in them of all children above the age of six. In fact, it was deemed unlawful to live in a place where there was no school and it was thought that such a city deserved to be destroyed.

The education that took place was marked by extreme care, wisdom, accuracy, and a moral and religious purpose as the end goal. The children could be gathered in synagogues or schoolhouses where they stood or sat in a semicircle, facing the teacher. The teacher was generally the *hazan*, the leader of the synagogue or was an officer of the synagogue. The teacher was to impart to the children the precious knowledge of the law with constant adaptation to their capacity, with unwearied patience, intense earnestness, strictness tempered by kindness, but above all, with the highest object of their training in view. He was to keep the children away from contact with vice; to train them to gentleness, even when the bitterest wrong had been received; to show sin in its repulsiveness, rather than to terrify by its consequences; to train to strict truthfulness; to avoid all that might lead to disagreeable or indelicate thoughts; and, to do all this without showing partiality, undue severity, or laxity of discipline. He was to teach with judicious study and work and with careful attention to thoroughness in acquiring knowledge. This was the ideal set before the teacher and made his office of high esteem in Israel.

It was held that the Bible should be the exclusive textbook up to ten years of age. From ten to fifteen years of age, the child was to learn the Mishnah, or traditional law. After this, the child would enter theological discussions which occupied time and attention in the higher academies of the rabbis. However, this progression was not always made. If the child had been taught and entered into Mishnaic studies and not shown any aptitude, there was little hope that was given to his future.

The *Mishnah* is a written collection of Jewish oral tradition that is reflective of how the Jews interpreted the Old Testament. After the Mishnah, there was supplementation to the oral traditions and so there were commentaries created called the *Gemara*. So, there was the Mishnah, which contained the oral tradition and then the Gemara, which was the commentary on the Mishnah, and these were combined to make the Talmud. There was and is both a Babylon Talmud and a Jerusalem Talmud. After this came the *midrash* which was a collection of interpretation on the books of the Bible.

The child would start his learning with the book of Leviticus which was done to teach the child of their guilt and the need of justification. After this, the child learned other parts of the Pentateuch, then the Prophets, and, finally, the Hagiographa, which included Ruth, Psalms, Job, Proverbs, Canticles, Lamentations, Ecclesiastes, Daniel, Esther, Ezra, and Chronicles. He would learn the Gemara which was the commentary on the Mishnah and would be taught the Talmud which was taught in the academies. There was care taken not to send a child too early to school and, thus, overwork them. Therefore, school hours were fixed and attendance shortened during the summer months.

The teaching in school would be aided by the services of the synagogue as well as the influences in the homelife. Not every home would have the whole Old Testament in Hebrew, but if there were some portions of the Word of God in the house, it would be the most cherished treasure of a pious household. The academies would hold copies of Holy Scripture and there was great care taken to preserve the integrity of the text and it was deemed unlawful to make copies of small portions of a book of Scripture. This was to prevent misquotes and misinterpretations in Scripture (1).

In summation, Nicodemus is an expert in Scripture and the law and has attained one of the highest positions in Jewish culture and religion. He is considered "the teacher of Israel." This title of being "the teacher of Israel" carries with it the full weight and force of what the Pharisees were teaching during the life and times of Jesus. Nicodemus was well-versed on teachings that circumcision was necessary for salvation. Nicodemus was well-versed on the pervasive and ubiquitous ceremonial handwashing, dish washing, pots and pans washing, and Mikvah purification immersion washing that was being taught. Nicodemus was well-versed on the restrictive extrabiblical Sabbath regulations that were taught. Nicodemus was "the teacher of Israel" who was on a crash course to learn about salvation and regeneration from Jesus.

John 3:2—*This man came to Jesus by night and said to him, "Rabbi, we know that you are a teacher come from God, for no one can do these signs that you do unless God is with him."*

Nicodemus, a member of the Sanhedrin, comes to Jesus in the cover of night. There may be many speculations made on why Nicodemus came by himself at night. Most likely it was because he was concerned over his salvation. Christ graciously welcomed Nicodemus. Though the Lord would go on and oppose the Pharisees numerous times, Christ still made time for a teacher coming at night. Nicodemus approaches Jesus in a respectful manner and calls Him "Rabbi." Nicodemus acknowledges that the Pharisees know that Jesus is a teacher that has come from God. Although Jesus was early on in His ministry, by this time Jesus had turned water into wine and had cleared the temple courts at the time of the Jewish Passover. The miracle of turning water into wine had never been performed. Therefore, Nicodemus knew that Jesus must have been sent by God given these signs.

John 3:3—*Jesus answered him, "Truly, truly, I say to you, unless one is born again he cannot see the kingdom of God."*

It seems odd that Jesus doesn't answer or respond to Nicodemus' greeting, but rather launches into a teaching and explanation of being born again. It is very likely that Jesus knew Nicodemus' heart and his thoughts since Jesus knew all people and knew what was in mankind (John 2:24–25). Therefore, it is reasonable to surmise that Nicodemus had come to Jesus because he had questions on salvation and perhaps even his own salvation. Jesus begins His teaching on regeneration by saying "Truly, truly," or rather, "Amen, amen." The lexicon describes *"amen"* by stating that *amen* means that "what is about to be said is sure and certain." It is also used at the beginning of a statement to introduce something of pivotal importance. As R. C. Sproul has said, "Whenever we read in the text of Scripture our Lord giving a statement that is prefaced by the double 'amen,' it is time to pay close attention and be ready to give our response with a double amen to it."

What does Jesus mean by being *born again*? In the original language, *born again* is *"gennethe anothen."* *Gennethe* is derived from *gennao* which means "to beget, or to bring forth." It is used to describe being born. The Greek word *anothen* can also be translated as "from above." When putting both words together, *born again* can also be translated as "born from above." The word *anothen* is referring to something coming from God or heaven. In James 1:17, the author says, "Every good and perfect gift is from **above**, coming from the Father of the heavenly light, who does not change like shifting shadows." Therefore, Jesus is referring to a birth that comes from above or from heaven.

The next phrase to dissect is *cannot see*. In the original language, it says *"ou dynatai idein."* The word *ou* is translated as "not." *Dynatai* is derived from the root word *dunamai* which means "to be able" or "to have power." The last word, *idein*, is derived from the root word *horao* which means to "see," "perceive," "discern," or, metaphorically, "to spiritually see with inward spiritual perception." The translation into English *"cannot see"* is a very good translation. Another way to accurately translate the whole phrase *"ou dynatai idein"* would be to say "has no power or ability to see or perceive."

As we mentioned earlier, the kingdom of God is the sphere of salvation over which God rules. Since it is God's kingdom, He is the King over all those who enter His kingdom. The kingdom of God and the kingdom of heaven carry the same meaning and describe the spiritual realm over which the Lord reigns as King.

So, let's put all these phrases together in verse 3. Jesus says, "Truly, truly, I say to you, unless someone is born again he cannot see the kingdom of God." I will take some liberty to say the same thing but in a different way that carries the same meaning:

- Most assuredly and most certainly, unless you are born from above, you have no power to see the sphere of salvation.
- This is the truth, unless you are born from above, you cannot spiritually understand how to enter the spiritual realm over which the Lord reigns.
- Pay attention to this important truth, unless you are born from above, you have no ability to see and understand how to be saved.Most assuredly and most certainly, unless you are born from above, you have no ability to see how to enter the kingdom of heaven through saving faith in Christ.

Notice here that being born from above is a necessity to enter the kingdom of God. Without spiritual regeneration, no man can see the call of repentance and faith (Mark 1:15). Also note that unless you are born from above, or have a spiritual rebirth, you can't see the kingdom of heaven and, thus, won't be able to enter the kingdom of heaven. Also note that this is a personal spiritual rebirth. Nicodemus should have asked himself the following questions: What ability do you have to be born from above? What role did you have in your physical birth? What role did you have in your conception? If you had no role in your physical birth or conception, what role do you have in your spiritual birth? The undeniable answer is that just as you had no role in your physical birth, you have no role in your spiritual birth.

Also pay attention to what Jesus just told Nicodemus. Nicodemus was at the highest religious level in Judaism and Jesus tells him that he must be born again before he can even perceive or see the kingdom of God. In other words, He's saying, "Nicodemus, all your religious achievement, all your education, all your knowledge, all your righteous works, all your ceremonies, all your Sabbaths, all your sacrifices, all your law keeping, all your prayers, all your Passovers, all your rituals, and all your efforts to enter into the kingdom amount to nothing. Nicodemus, weren't you paying attention to John the Baptist's message? You need to start all over again because what you have falls short. God is not impressed by your religious achievements. All your years of apostate Judaism is worth nothing. If you want to enter the kingdom of God, you need to start all over and be born from above." This is what Jesus is telling Nicodemus.

Also take care to note that if you have not been born from above, you are spiritually dead. If you have not been born from above, you will not have spiritual life when you die.

John 3:4—*Nicodemus said to him, "How can a man be born when he is old? Can he enter a second time into his mother's womb and be born?"*

Nicodemus understands what Jesus just said. Nicodemus understands that Jesus is using a physical example to explain a spiritual reality. Nicodemus understands that it is impossible to be physically born a second time. There is no example of anyone ever being physically born again so Nicodemus knows that physical rebirth is impossible. Therefore, Jesus' example is showing Nicodemus that if physical rebirth is impossible, how much more impossible is it to be born from above? How can a man make physical rebirth happen? Likewise, what can a man do to be born from above? What prayer can he pray? What sacrament can he partake in? What law can he keep? What good work can he do? What ceremonial or sacramental washing can he partake in? What Sabbath observance can he observe? He could also ask more questions about physical rebirth: What role did he play in his first birth? Did he have any say when he was conceived? Did he have any say what day he was born? Did he have any say in his gender? Did he have any say on how long he stayed in the womb?

When looking into Scripture, surely Nicodemus would know Psalm 139:13–15, "For you created my innermost parts; you wove me in my mother's womb. I will give thanks to You, because I am awesomely and wonderfully made; wonderful are your works, and my soul knows it very well. My frame was not hidden from You when I was made in secret, and skillfully formed in the depths of the earth. Your eyes have seen my formless substance; and in Your book were written all the days that were ordained for me, when as yet there was not one of them." So, just as Nicodemus had no part in his physical birth, he would surely have no part in a spiritual birth. Jesus is showing that being born from above is simply a monergistic work of God that man has no control over and Nicodemus understands the impossibility of rebirth by Jesus' question.

John 3:5—*Jesus answered, "truly, truly, I say to you, unless one is born of water and the Spirit, he cannot enter the kingdom of God."*

Jesus is about to make another statement that is of critical importance. As we learned earlier, it is time to pay attention because what He is about to say is an essential truth as triggered by the double amen. Jesus says, "Unless someone is born of water and the Spirit, he cannot enter the kingdom of God." Since we have taken time to understand what the kingdom of God is, we need to understand what it means to be born of water and the Spirit. Commentaries from different theologians and denominations look to this passage as clear evidence that this is a reference to Christian baptism. This is the furthest thing from the mind of Christ.

In fact, ceremonial washings during this time were widespread. There were washings for hands, cups, pots, copper vessels, and dining couches (Mark 7:1–7). The Mishnah contains several regulations on handwashing such as how much water can be used, what kind of vessel could be used to pour water over one's hands, how to handle cases of doubtful impurity for handwashing, and more. Not only these, ritual pools called *mikvahs* were used for ceremonial cleanliness. There were regulations on how much water was needed to make a mikvah, what type of water made a mikvah, what happened if objects fell into a mikvah, rules for immersion, and more. Jesus was not insinuating that regeneration was brought on by some sort of ceremonial washing. May it never be! Nicodemus would not have been thinking that he just needed to undergo one more ceremony or ritual, or perform one more good work, as Jesus is emphasizing being born from above. Nicodemus would have been very familiar with all the Old Testament water purification rituals. Nicodemus would have been very familiar with the Mikvah water purification rituals and ceremonial cleansings. Nicodemus would have been very familiar with the Mikvah purification rituals as these relate to converting to Judaism.

Jesus has just gotten done explaining that you must be born from above to see the kingdom of God and Nicodemus understands that this second birth is out of his control. Jesus is about to double down on the emphasis of the new birth being a monergistic act of God. John the Baptist said in Luke 3:16, "John answered them all, 'I baptize you with water. But one who is more powerful than I will come, the straps of whose sandals I am not worthy to untie. He will baptize you with the Holy Spirit and fire.'" In fact,

Matthew, Mark, Luke, John, Jesus, John the Baptist, and Peter all note that Christ is the only one who can baptize with the Holy Spirit and that man can only baptize with water (Matthew 3:11–12; Mark 1:8; Luke 3:16; John 1:31–33; 3:8; 7:38–39; 14:15–17, 26; 15:26; 16:7; Acts 1:4–5, 2:17–18, 10:44–48, 11:16).

So, what is Jesus trying to say? Remember that Nicodemus was advanced in Judaism and, as Jesus said in verse 10, "You are the teacher of Israel." Jesus says, "Nicodemus, you are *the* teacher," using a definite article. Jesus says, "You are not *a* teacher," which is an indefinite article, but *"the"* teacher. Jesus is telling Nicodemus to follow along. Jesus is saying, "You should know what I'm saying when I say, 'born of water and the spirit.'" Jesus is pointing Nicodemus to the New Covenant promise of Ezekiel 36. Although the scripture of Ezekiel 36 is being spoken to Israel, it is true for every believer. Ezekiel 36:24–27 says, "For I will take you from the nations, and gather you from all the lands; and I will bring you into your own land. Then I will sprinkle clean **water** on you, and you will be clean; I will cleanse you from all your filthiness and from all your idols. Moreover, I will give you a new heart and put a new spirit within you; and I will remove the heart of stone from your flesh and give you a heart of flesh. And I will put my **Spirit** within you and bring it about that you walk in My statutes, and are careful and follow My ordinances." This is most certainly where Jesus is pointing Nicodemus.

Nicodemus would have and should have been aware of this passage of Scripture as it pointed to Israel's restoration, and he should have been aware of the personal pronouns in this portion of Scripture. In these three short verses, the LORD uses the personal pronoun *"I"* seven times. He is indicating that this salvation will strictly be a work of God. This work of salvation will be a one-sided affair. The LORD God is going to perform a mighty act of salvation for His name's sake. To understand Jesus' statement of being born of water and the Spirit, it is important to understand Ezekiel 36:24–27.

Ezekiel 36:24 – *I will take you from the nations and gather you from all the countries and bring you into your own land.*

In this section, the LORD is pointing to separation or holiness. This is to say that when God justifies, God also sanctifies. It is to say when God gives the man the gift of faith and repentance and brings him through the narrow gate, God immediately places that man on the narrow road (Matthew 7:13–14). Let us firmly remember Ezekiel 36:23 where the LORD says, "And I will vindicate the holiness of My great name which has been profaned among the nations, which you have profaned among them. Then the nations will know that I am the LORD, declares the LORD God, when I show Myself holy among you in their sight." When God regenerates and saves a man, He is proven holy among men and the nations. That is to say that the salvific work of God is so holy and amazing that, although unregenerate man may not fully understand the salvation that took place, they will marvel and awe at the transforming and regenerative work of God who puts the life of God in the soul of a man. It is to say that God always acts first! You can almost hear Jesus saying, "Nicodemus, aren't you familiar with Ezekiel 16:1–8?"

"The word of the Lord came to me: 'Son of man, confront Jerusalem with her detestable practices and say, "This is what the Sovereign Lord says to Jerusalem: Your ancestry and birth were in the land of the Canaanites; your father was an Amorite and your mother a Hittite. On the day you were born your cord was not cut, nor were you washed with water to make you clean, nor were you rubbed with salt or wrapped in cloths. No one looked on you with pity or had compassion enough to do any of these things for you. Rather, you were thrown out into the open field, for on the day you were born you were despised." 'Then I passed by and saw you kicking about in your blood, and as you lay there in your blood I said to you, "Live!" I made you grow like a plant of the field. You grew and developed and entered puberty. Your breasts had formed and your hair had grown,

THE GOSPEL CALL • 139

yet you were stark naked.' "Later I passed by, and when I looked at you and saw that you were old enough for love, I spread the corner of my garment over you and covered your naked body. I gave you my solemn oath and entered into a covenant with you, declares the Sovereign Lord, and you became mine."

It is as if Jesus is telling Nicodemus, "It has always been about God acting on His own initiative and will." It is as if Jesus is saying, "You've never done anything to earn my favor. Nicodemus, don't you see that you were not a nation, until I made you a nation? Nicodemus, don't you remember when I spoke to Elijah and told him that I have reserved 7,000 in Israel—all whose knees have not bowed down to Baal and whose mouths have not kissed him (1 Kings 19:18)? Nicodemus, don't you know that I'm the one who set apart Israel for Myself? Nicodemus, don't you see that I alone separate men unto Myself?"

Ezekiel 36:25—I will sprinkle clean water on you, and you shall be clean from all your uncleannesses, and from all your idols I will cleanse you.

Once again, notice the personal pronoun of *"I."* **I** will sprinkle clean water on you and **I** will cleanse you. The question to ask is: What is this reference to water? It is a reference to forgiveness. After David had been confronted for his sin of adultery and murder by the prophet Nathan, he penned Psalm 51, which gives us insight into this water and cleansing reference. In Psalm 51:1–2, he says, "Be gracious to me, God, according to Your faithfulness; According to the greatness of Your compassion, wipe out my wrongdoings. Wash me thoroughly from my guilt and cleanse me from my sin." In verse 7, he says, "Purify me with hyssop, and I will be clean; cleanse me, and I will be whiter than snow." No theologian would *exposit*, or try to reason, that David is asking the LORD for a bath, a shower, or a ceremonial washing. No, the washing that David is asking for is the washing away and cleansing of sins. He is asking for personal forgiveness from the LORD. He is asking that the LORD would not look at his sins but turn away from them and forgive them. He is asking the LORD for mercy and compassion and not to deal with him according to justice. He is also asking to be cleansed. In the Hebrew, this word is *taher*, which means "to be clean or pure." In context, David is saying, "Cleanse me and purge me from my immorality. Only You can make me morally clean. Only You can cleanse my murderous and adulterous heart. I don't need a physical bath, LORD! I need You to cleanse the filth in my heart and forgive me."

In Psalm 51:10, David cries out for the same thing, "Create in me a clean heart, God, and renew a steadfast spirit within me." Once again paraphrasing David, "LORD, I have no ability to change my heart. I have no ability to keep Your laws. LORD, without You cleansing my heart and renewing my spirit, I am hopeless." In verse 25 of Ezekiel, the LORD is saying this very thing. The LORD is saying that He is the one who will act to forgive sins. He is the one who will purify us from our sins. He is the one who will cleanse us from our filthiness and idols. Note here that this is not just a reference to forgiveness of sins. This is also a promise to purify us morally from our sins and idols. Again, what the LORD is saying is that this cleansing and purification is not just forgiveness of sins, but a continual work of God to rid one's life of sin. Nicodemus should have known this. You can almost hear Jesus saying to Nicodemus, "Nicodemus, don't you know that it is God who forgives sins? Nicodemus, don't you know that it is God who cleanses people from their sins? Don't you know that unless God cleanses someone from the inside, he cannot be clean before God? Nicodemus, don't you know that external water cannot take away the stain of sin, but only God can remove the stain of sin? Nicodemus, won't you learn from David and see that the cleansing you really need is from the heart? Nicodemus, God is the one who sprinkles the clean water and who cleanses you."

Ezekiel 36:26—*And I will give you a new heart, and a new spirit I will put within you. And I will remove the heart of stone from your flesh and give you a heart of flesh.*

Let's remember that Jesus just said to Nicodemus that you must be born of water and the Spirit. Verse 25 captures the water and verse 27 captures the Spirit but sandwiched in between the water and the Spirit is verse 26 that talks about the LORD giving a new heart and a new spirit. So, what does this mean? When the LORD says He will give a new heart and a new spirit, He is saying that He isn't going to help man be a better person, or become more moral, or to help him love Him just a little more. No, He is saying that He is going to change man's very nature and who man is. Oftentimes, the heart and the spirit encapsulate man's intellect, emotions/affections, and will (i.e., his whole being). What the LORD is saying is that He is going to change man's intellect so man will know the LORD. He will change man's emotions and affections so that man's affections will be toward the LORD and what the LORD loves. What the LORD hates, man will hate and what the LORD loves, man will love. The LORD will also change man's will so that man's disposition will be inclined to do the will of the LORD.

What is a heart of stone? A *heart of stone* is an inanimate object. A heart that has no life. You can kick a stone, you can shock a stone, you can scream at a stone, but the stone will not respond. The heart of stone does not respond to divine stimuli or God's Word. A *heart of flesh* is a heart that is alive. The heart of flesh is responsive. The heart of flesh has a pulse. The heart of flesh responds to divine stimuli or God's Word. What then is the spirit? The *spirit* is the innermost part of man. In Genesis 6:5, it says, "The LORD saw how great the wickedness of the human race had become on the earth, and that every inclination of the thoughts of the human heart was only evil all the time." That is the inclination of man. That is man's heart and spirit. Man's heart and spirit is only evil and inclined toward evil all the time. In Jeremiah 13:23, the LORD says, "Can an Ethiopian change his skin or a leopard its spots? Neither can you do good who are accustomed to doing evil." Once again, the LORD is saying man cannot change his evil disposition no more than a leopard or an Ethiopian can change his skin. It is not possible. The LORD says of man's heart in Jeremiah 17:9, "The heart is deceitful above all things and beyond cure. Who can understand it?" Once again, verse 26 is sandwiched between water and the spirit and Jesus is drawing Nicodemus to this sovereign act of God which changes a man's very being and imparts spiritual life.

Ontology is the study of being or the nature of being. A man will follow his nature. A pig will always lay in its filth. A bird will fly south when winter comes. A man will always choose evil because that is his nature. The changing of one's being is only accomplished by the sovereign work of God. Man can't change his nature. In fact, Ezekiel 11:19–20, 36:24–27 and Jeremiah 24:7, 31:33–34, 32:38–40 capture this very idea of God changing man's intellect, emotions and affections, will, and nature so man is inclined to repent and trust in Jesus Christ. Notice the "I will" statements which highlight the act of God monergistically acting on His own to save. Notice the changes to the "spirit," "heart," and "mind" which highlight God changing man from the inside. Notice the new covenant language of *"they will be my people, and I shall be their God"* which explains how God makes a right relationship with man; by changing the inside of a man:

*And **I will give them one heart,** and **put a new spirit within them**. And **I will remove the heart of stone from their flesh** and **give them a heart of flesh**, so that they will walk in My statutes, and keep My ordinances and do them. Then they will be My people, and I shall be their God (Ezekiel 11:19–20). **I will also give them a heart to know Me,** for I am the LORD; and they will be My people, and I will be their God, for they will return to Me wholeheartedly (Jeremiah 24:7). They shall be My people, and I will be their God;*

and ***I will give them one heart and one way,*** *so that they will fear Me always, for their own good and for the good of their children after them.* ***I will make an everlasting covenant*** *with them that* ***I will not turn away from them, to do them good; and, I will put the fear of Me in their hearts,*** *so that they will not turn away from Me (Jeremiah 32:38–40). For* ***I will take you from the nations,*** *and gather you from all the lands; and,* ***I will bring you into your own land.*** *Then,* ***I will sprinkle clean water on you, and you will be clean;*** *I will cleanse you from all your filthiness and from all your idols. Moreover,* ***I will give you a new heart and put a new spirit within you;*** *and,* ***I will remove the heart of stone from your flesh and give you a heart of flesh.*** *And,* ***I will put My Spirit within you and bring it about that you walk in My statutes, and are careful and follow my ordinances*** *(Ezekiel 36:24–27).* ***For this is the covenant which I will make with the house of Israel*** *after those days, "Declares the LORD: '****I will put My law within them and write it on their heart;*** *and* ***I will be their God,*** *and they shall be My people. They will not teach again, each one his neighbor and each one his brother,' saying, "Know the LORD," for they will all know Me, from the least of them to the greatest of them,' declares the LORD, "for* ***I will forgive their wrongdoing,*** *and* ***their sin I will no longer remember"*** *(Jeremiah 31:33–34).*

It is as if Jesus is telling Nicodemus, "Nicodemus, don't you know that in your fallen nature, you are only prone to evil? Nicodemus, don't you remember that your heart is only wicked all the time? Nicodemus, don't you understand that your heart is deceitful and beyond cure? Nicodemus, God needs to remove your heart of stone from your flesh and give you a heart of flesh and give you a new spirit. Nicodemus, you don't perform this work, God does it. Nicodemus, don't you remember that God is the one that writes His law on your heart and mind? Nicodemus, don't you realize that when you receive this new heart and new spirit, God's laws will be written on them as well? Nicodemus, how do you earn getting a new heart and a new spirit? Nicodemus, don't you see that the old covenant was written on stone tablets and the promised new covenant will be written on the heart of flesh? Nicodemus, don't you know that it is God who must completely change your intellect, affections, and will?"

Ezekiel 36:27—And I will put my Spirit within you, and cause you to walk in my statues and be careful to obey my rules.

As part of this new covenant promise, the LORD promises that He will put His Spirit in us to walk in His ways. So let's recap. The LORD is saying that He will forgive our sins. The LORD will cleanse us from our impurities and sins. The LORD will write His law on our heart and mind. The LORD will give us a new heart and spirit and completely change us. Finally, the LORD will give us His Spirit so that we will be careful and able to obey Him. It is as if Jesus is telling Nicodemus, "Nicodemus, it is God who forgives our sins. It is God who cleanses us from our sin. It is God who gives us a new heart, new spirit, and completely changes our nature and will. It is God who writes His law on our heart. It is God who writes His law on our mind. It is God who gives us a heart of flesh. It is God who puts His Spirit in us. It is God who gives a heart to fear Him. It is God who gives us the new heart to return to Him wholeheartedly. Nicodemus, don't you know that salvation is from the LORD and not from ceremonies, rituals, law observance, ceremonial washings, and the like? Nicodemus, it is God who causes you to be born from above. It is God who gives you the gift of faith. It is God who gives you the gift of repentance. It is all about God monergistically saving man." Jesus is emphasizing that salvation and regeneration are the sovereign monergistic work of God to Nicodemus and He seeks to remind Nicodemus of this by drawing him to the new covenant promise in Ezekiel 36.

John 3:6—*That which is born of the flesh is flesh, and that which is born of the Spirit is spirit.*

It is as if Jesus is telling Nicodemus that he needs to go back and study his theology of man. Jesus is telling Nicodemus to go back and study man's total depravity and inability to please God on his own merits. You can almost hear Jesus telling Nicodemus to recall the depravity of man.

- Ecclesiastes 7:20—Surely there is not a righteous man on earth who does good and never sins.
- Psalm 51:5—Behold, I was brought forth in iniquity, and in sin did my mother conceive me.
- Jeremiah 17:9—The heart is deceitful above all things, and desperately sick; who can understand it?
- Psalm 14:2–3—The LORD looks down from heaven on the children of man, to see if there are any who understand, who seek after God. They have all turned aside; together they have become corrupt; there is none who does good, not even one.
- Genesis 6:5—The LORD saw the wickedness of man was great in the earth, and that every intention of the thoughts of his heart was only evil continually.

Jesus is telling Nicodemus that the only thing that man can produce is flesh and wickedness. Man can do nothing that produces any spiritual life. If flesh can only produce flesh, then flesh can only produce sin. Flesh can only produce spiritual death. Flesh is incapable of producing righteousness. Jesus also says that the Spirit gives birth to spirit. Once again, Nicodemus should have known what this meant, and Jesus seeks to remind him that only by the Spirit can man live. Only by the Spirit can man have spiritual life. Judaism had reached a terrible level of legalism and rituals. Jesus shut the door to works, actions, rituals, and externality, which were emphasized by the Pharisees. Jesus declared that these things did not give you entrance into the kingdom of God. Entrance to the kingdom of God was by the regenerating work of God the Holy Spirit.

John 3:7—*Do not marvel that I said to you, 'You must be born again.'*

Jesus reiterates the same truth to Nicodemus that He stated in verse 3. In verse 3, Jesus says you must be born from above to even see the kingdom of God. In other words, you can't even see how to be reconciled with God and be saved unless you have been born from above. Jesus is saying this to Nicodemus a second time as He is emphasizing this important point to teach Nicodemus of the sovereign monergistic work of God. In fact, He tells Nicodemus, "You should not be surprised." The original language translates this word *thaumases* or *thaumazo*, which means "to wonder at, be amazed (i.e., astonished out of one's senses, awestruck), or to regard with amazement." In other words, this teaching of being born from above should not have been a new or amazing teaching.

Let's also notice in this verse that Jesus says, "You must be born again." Jesus is saying that "you" must be born from above again. There are two important words here. The first word of importance is *you*. Here, Jesus is saying this is a personal birth from above. This is not a group birth but a personal birth from above that must occur. Just as you came into the world at a certain location and at a certain time, so it is with your spiritual birth. Unless a man is born from above, he will not enter or see the kingdom of God. Second, Jesus says, "You **must** be born again." The original word *dei* means that it is necessary. This second birth is a necessity. Without a second birth, you have no spiritual life. Without a second birth, you are dead in trespasses, alienated from God, and an enemy of the Lord. Jesus is emphasizing the importance and necessity of the new birth to enter the kingdom of God.

John 3:8—*The wind blows where it wishes, and you hear its sound, but you do not know where it comes from or where it goes. So it is within everyone who is born of the Spirit.*

If we are closely following along with Jesus, we see that He is saying you must be born from above which is something that God controls and not man (v. 3). Jesus is saying that we must be born of water and the Spirit which is in reference to Ezekiel 36, where God is sovereignly acting to give man a new heart, a new spirit, and put His Spirit within man (v. 5). He has stated that man in his depraved state can only produce flesh and sin, but the Spirit gives birth to spirit and life (v. 6). Jesus states again the necessity of being born from above to Nicodemus (v. 7). Thus far, we have Jesus making four statements that man's entrance into the kingdom of God is a work from God the Holy Spirit where the Holy Spirit monergistically acts to change man and give him spiritual life. Jesus is going to give another earthly analogy to explain a spiritual reality. This time, He chooses the wind as a metaphor. Jesus' first statement is that the wind blows where it pleases. This is to draw Nicodemus to the following understanding:

- What can you do to start the wind?
- What can you do to stop the wind?
- What can you do to influence the wind?
- What can you do to control the wind?

The answer to these questions is nothing. Just as man cannot control the wind, so man cannot control the Spirit. There is nothing done by man to influence the wind. There is nothing done by man to control the wind. There is nothing done by man to command the wind. The Spirit operates freely and totally by Divine will. This is Jesus' first point.

The second point Jesus makes with the wind metaphor is that you can hear its sound, but you cannot tell where it comes from or where it is going. So, it is with everyone born of the Spirit. Here Jesus is saying that when the Spirit operates, you hear His sound. Another way of restating this is, when the Spirit operates, you will know that there was work done by the Spirit. When the Spirit operates, it will be obvious that a work of God was done to change a man. When the Spirit operates, you will see a man with a new nature and new affections. You will not know where the Spirit came from or went, but it will be obvious that someone was operated on by the Spirit. Jesus' analogy of the way the wind works being analogous to the Spirit cannot be mistaken. He is emphasizing the monergistic work of God and the transformational outcome. We can't control the wind or the Spirit, but we will be able to tell when the Spirit has been at work. Just like we can't control a tornado or a hurricane, we will see when there has been a tornado or a hurricane and we will see the evidence of it. Everyone born of the Spirit has undergone a sovereign monergistic work of God the Holy Spirit and, where God the Holy Spirit has acted, it will be clear that there will be a person with a new heart, a new spirit, and the Spirit of God working in that person.

John 3:9–10—*Nicodemus said to him, "How can these things be?" Jesus answered him, "Are you the teacher of Israel and yet you do not understand these things?"*

Nicodemus has still not understood the meaning of the second birth and Jesus is unveiling the spiritual depth to which Israel and one of Israel's premier teachers has fallen. A better translation of *"You are Israel's teacher"* could be as follows, "You are **the** teacher of Israel and these things you do not know?" This is a definite article. Jesus is not saying you are *a* teacher, but *the* teacher. In other words, Nicodemus is the premier teacher of Judaism in Israel, and he has not grasped the understanding of the new birth and God's Spirit bringing life to spiritually dead men. Nicodemus should have known the new covenant promise in Ezekiel 36. Nicodemus should have known the new covenant promise in Jeremiah 33 where God writes His laws on man's heart and mind. Nicodemus should have known the total depravity of man's sinful state. Nicodemus should have known that man's good works are like filthy rags. Nicodemus should have known that man can't give himself spiritual life. Jesus is telling "the" teacher in Israel that he needs to start all over because he doesn't understand the sovereign saving work of God and needs to start over and be born from above to enter the kingdom of God. Jesus is telling Nicodemus that salvation has always been from God and not from man. How far Israel had fallen. No wonder Jesus was moved with compassion in Matthew 9:36 as He saw that His covenant people were harassed and helpless, like sheep without a shepherd. We can, thus, come away with a definition of *regeneration* which is: **the sovereign monergistic work of God the Holy Spirit in giving spiritual life to spiritually dead and sinful man so that man is enabled to repent and respond in saving faith to Jesus Christ.**

John 3:16—*For God so loved the world, that he gave his only Son, that whoever believes in him should not perish but have eternal life.*

Jesus would continue to instruct "the teacher of Israel." Pharisaical Judaism was ceremonial, legalistic, ritualistic, cold, mechanical, and unloving. Jesus would further instruct Nicodemus on the character of God and salvation.

First, we see that God the Father was the one to act out of love. God the Father didn't wait for man to come up with a plan of salvation. No, God the Father was the one who would initiate and execute this plan of salvation. God the Father was the sovereign creator and author of the gospel. Paul would say it this way in Romans 1:1 that this gospel was from God and not from man where he says, "Paul, a servant of Christ Jesus, called to be an apostle, set apart for the gospel of God." The gospel is God the Father's. This gospel was determined in eternity past between the Godhead of the Father, Son, and Holy Spirit.

Second, we see the indescribable love of God the Father. God the Father loved the world. This is the very world that has rebelled against Him. This is the same God who **hates** sin and those who practice it (Psalm 5:5). This is the same God that **abhors** the bloodthirsty and sinful man (Psalm 5:6). This is the same God that is **angry** with wicked sinners (Psalm 7:11). This is the same God that is ready to **destroy** wicked and unrepentant sinners (Psalm 7:12–13). This is the same God that **hates** the wicked who love violence and sin (Psalm 11:5). This is the same God that considers sin as being in **warfare with Him** (James 4:4). This is the same God that considers sin an **abomination** (Proverbs 22:12). This is the same God that considers sin as **evil** as well as everyone who commits sin (Psalm 7:9). God the Father's soul hates the wicked. In fact, there was nothing redeemable in man which would elicit love from God the Father. There was nothing redeemable in man that God should love. This love of God the Father was a predetermined love that occurred in eternity past and will continue in eternity future for God does not change like shifting shadows (James 1:17). This love of God the Father is lavish (1 John 3:1). This love of God the Father is rich (Ephesians 2:4). This love of God the Father is described as loving kindness (Titus 3:4). This love of God the Father endures forever (Psalm 136). God determined in eternity past to love the very ones who rebelled against him, waged war against him, violated his law, rebelled against his commands, and proved that they so hated God that they would crucify His Son.

Third, let's note that God loved the world. God didn't just love the Jews. God the Father loved a great multitude of people from every nation, from every tribe, and from every language (Revelation 7:9). God's love wasn't just confined to the Jews or even the elite Jews who were advanced in knowledge. God's love extended past the Jews. Jesus loved and came to save the Jew, the Greek, the circumcised, the uncircumcised, the barbarian, the Scythian, the slave, the free, women, children, the Samaritan, and all mankind (John 4, Colossians 3:11).

Fourth, note that God so loved the world that He gave His one-of-a-kind Son. The word *Only Begotten* has been translated from *monogenés* which properly means "one and only" or "one of a kind," literally, "one of a class and the only of its kind." Jesus is the "only one-of-a-kind" Son of God. God the Father didn't give the world another animal sacrifice. God the Father didn't give more rules that needed to be followed in order for man to save himself. No, God the Father gave His Son, His only Son whom He had loved from all eternity past. God the Father gave His only Son whom He loved and with whom He was well pleased (Matthew 3:17, 17:5; Mark 1:11). A parent who loves their child knows the pain of what it would be like to give up just one of their children. A parent is sinful and their children are sinful. God the Father who is perfect (Matthew 5:48) gave His only Son who was also perfect (John 5:17–18).

Fifth, note too that God so loved the world that He gave up His one and only Son to die and suffer His wrath in man's place. When Jesus tells Nicodemus that God gave His only Son, this is a reference to John 3:14 where Moses lifted up the snake for the Israelites. Just as the snake was lifted up on a pole for all to look at the snake and live, so Christ would be lifted up on the cross as a substitutionary sacrifice for the sins of men so they may live and not perish. God didn't unload a rifle firing squad on His Son. God didn't unload a nuclear bomb on His Son. God didn't unload the full heat of the sun on His Son. No, God unloaded something far more terrifying than all these combined. God unloaded His full unbridled wrath on His Only Begotten Son. God the Father cursed His perfect and beloved Son on the cross as if Christ was the vile, loathsome, wicked, malicious, and abhorrent sinner (Galatians 3:13). Upon the cross, God the Father poured out His white-hot wrath on His Son (Matthew 26:39). Upon the cross, the Father poured out His full furious and fiery wrath on the Lord Jesus Christ and turned His face away from His Son (Matthew 27:46).

In Matthew 25:31-46, Jesus explains how everyone will be judged. In this explanation, He states that the goats, or rather, those who refuse to repent and put their faith in Christ are cursed and the sheep, or rather, those who repent and put their faith in Christ are blessed. So how does the Lord treat the unrepentant and unbelieving goats? He says this of the goats in Matthew 25:41, "Depart from me, **you cursed**, into the eternal fire prepared for the devil and his angels." In Galatians 3:13 it says, "Christ redeemed us from the curse of the law by **becoming a curse for us** – for it is written, 'Cursed is everyone who is hanged on a tree'". When Jesus Christ was on the cross, He was treated as a cursed sinner. The punishment for sin is hell. Christ suffered this punishment on the cross for the elect. Only an eternal God could suffer an eternal punishment. Only the Son of God and Son of Man could propitiate the righteous wrath of God the Father. One cannot even comprehend the wrath that was poured out on the Son. Just one lustful intent is enough to damn a man's soul and cast him into hell for all eternity (Matthew 5:28). Upon the cross, Jesus absorbed the full fiery wrath from His Father for the sins of all who would be saved. If one sin is not paid for, man would remain damned. If one sin was left unpunished, man would remain cursed. If one sin was not propitiated, man would remain indebted and damned. If one sin was not atoned for, man would remain condemned. Imagine if a father could take the sun, which at its core is 27 million degrees Fahrenheit, and lift it up on cast it down on his son to crush him and then turn his back on his child as the child was left to suffer. Imagine the father crushing his son with the full weight and heat of the sun, turning his back and saying, "I cannot and will not look upon my beloved son with favor as I curse him and crush him." This is but a pathetic example of the wrath that the Father poured out on His Son. The Father's wrath for sin is far greater than we will ever know. The purposeful, eternal, rich and bountiful love that was demonstrated by God the Father to curse His Son on the cross in place for sinners who rebel against Him is unfathomable to the human mind.

Sixth, let us see that God the Father offered up His Son that whoever would believe unto Him should not eternally perish but have eternal life. Unlike the harsh, cold, and burdensome rules the Pharisees laid upon the Jews, the Father gave His Son that whoever would have faith in His Son should not suffer the punishment of hell but would have a new quantity of life and a new quality of life which is eternal life. Unlike the harsh rules that the Pharisees gave the people which could never save, God gave His Son that whoever would repent and have faith in Him should be saved. Nicodemus' heart should have been plowed by the preaching of John the Baptist. Nicodemus should have paid attention to John's message that works and self-righteousness needed to be brought down low and the sins must be confessed and repented of in preparation to receive the Messiah through faith.

As Jesus would close His dialogue with Nicodemus, He would say the following in John 3:19–21, "And this is the judgment: the light has come into the world, and people loved the darkness rather than the light because their works were evil. For everyone who does wicked things hates the light and does not come to the light, lest his works should be exposed. But whoever does what is true comes to the light, so that it may be clearly seen that his works have been carried out in God." As Jesus would claim to be the Light of the World later in His ministry (John 8:12), He would also ominously claim that those who would not come to Him for salvation remained in darkness.

As we close this section, we see how Nicodemus "the teacher of Israel," needed much instruction. Nicodemus needed instruction on the new birth or regeneration. Nicodemus needed correction on the depravity of man's sin. Nicodemus needed correction on where salvation came from. Nicodemus needed correction on the terms of salvation, repentance, and faith. Nicodemus needed correction on the attributes of God. Nicodemus needed much humbling. "The teacher of Israel" needed to humble himself before the Lord, for the Lord had showed Nicodemus his error. Nicodemus should have been afflicted for leading Israel astray.

Did James learn a lesson on regeneration? Was James convinced that regeneration was a sovereign monergistic work of God to give spiritual life to spiritually dead men? James 1:18 helps us answer this question where James says, "Of his own will he **brought us forth** by the word of truth, that we should be a kind of firstfruits of his creatures." The word *brought forth* is from a compound word, *apokueó*, with *apo* meaning "away from" and *kueó* meaning "to be pregnant" or "to conceive." Properly, *apokueó* means "to give birth." How is one given the new birth? James would say that it is by God's "word of truth" or God's Word. It is the gospel that is powerful to save. How do we know that James knew this was regeneration or the new birth? James states that we were brought forth by the word of truth "that we should be a kind of firstfruits of his creatures." Paul would call such a person a "new creation." James would know that a new creation is the result of regeneration. Therefore, we see that James was also influenced by the Lord's teaching on the new birth, being born again, or regeneration.

Nicodemus, the Teacher of Israel, Becomes the Humble Follower of Jesus

Nicodemus, who was a Pharisee, was part of the religious sect that Jesus came into conflict many times during His ministry.

The Pharisees took issue with the works and the teachings of Jesus. The Pharisees would remain unrepentant and unbelieving. Their hearts were hardened, their necks were stiffened, their eyes were dulled, their ears were waxed, their intentions turned murderous, their speech turned to deceit, their words turned to blasphemy, their pride remained high, their sin was justified, and their self-exaltation could not be exchanged for self-denial. Nicodemus would have a very different sovereign outcome then his contemporaries. But first, let's look at the path of unconverted Pharisees. This will help us see how the Pharisees would not be humbled but were determined to remain exalted. This will help us see how a high-ranking Jewish leader left his place of exaltation in Jewish culture and humbled himself before the Lord.

The obstinance of the Pharisees started right away during John the Baptist's ministry where the Pharisees rejected the need for repentance (Matthew 3:1–9; Luke 3:3–17, 7:30). The Pharisees thought Jesus was a blasphemer as Jesus proclaimed to be the Son of Man who had authority to forgive sins. The Pharisees refused to be humbled and repent when Jesus substantiated this claim by making a paralytic man walk (Luke 5:17–26). The Pharisees grumbled when Jesus ate with sinners and tax collectors, but Jesus reminded them that He came to call sinners to repentance and those who are well needed no physician (Luke 5:27–32). The Pharisees were corrected by Jesus on their misunderstanding of fasting and Jesus warned through a parable that those who had acquired a taste for old covenant ceremonies would not want to give it up for His teaching (Luke 5:33–39). The Pharisees were angered over Jesus healing a man on the Sabbath, breaking their extrabiblical Sabbath laws, and Jesus' claims to deity that they desired to kill Him rather than pay attention to His divine work and teaching (John 5:1–47).

The Pharisees were corrected by Jesus on their understanding of the Sabbath when Jesus rebuked them for their extrabiblical Sabbath regulations, illustrated that mercy and compassion were greater than ceremony and ritual. Jesus would then claim that He was Lord of the Sabbath, or rather, God (Luke 6:1–5). The Pharisees angered the Lord when Jesus demonstrated that it was lawful to do good on the Sabbath by healing a man with a withered hand. However, instead of being repentant, they plotted on how to kill Him (Mark 3:1–6). Simon, who was a Pharisee, saw a sinful woman who was transformed and forgiven, and that God was ready and willing to save repentant and mournful sinners who loved Him rather than the self-righteous (Luke 7:36–50).

The Pharisees accused Jesus of driving out demons by Beelzebul when Jesus healed a demon-possessed man who was blind and mute. Jesus then accused the Pharisees of blasphemy against the Holy Spirit by attributing the works of God to the works of Satan (Matthew 12:22–32). The Pharisees asked for a sign from heaven from Jesus rather than believing the teaching and works which clearly demonstrated that Jesus was the Messiah. Jesus pronounced judgment on them for such unbelief (Matthew 12:38–45). The Pharisees claimed Jesus healed a demon-possessed mute man by the prince of demons even though the crowds saw that nothing had ever been done like this in Israel (Matthew 9:32–34). The Pharisees were rebuked by Jesus for their extrabiblical ceremonial washings, for neglecting the commands of God, for false worship, for hypocrisy, and for being false teachers (Matthew 15:1–20). The Pharisees again tested the Lord by asking Him for a sign from heaven even though His works and teaching validated His claims to being the Messiah. Jesus declared them spiritually blind and an adulterous generation (Matthew 16:1–4).

The Pharisees wanted to kill and arrest Jesus and would not be convinced that Jesus was the Christ when Jesus began teaching at the Feast of Booths. Jesus claimed that He was from the Father and amazed the crowds (John 7:1–52). At the Feast of Booths, the tension would escalate between Jesus and the Pharisees where the Pharisees refused to believe Jesus' testimony and claims.

THE GOSPEL CALL • 157

Jesus claimed that the Pharisees were from the devil because of their intent to kill Him. He claimed to be God and the Pharisees tried to stone Jesus (John 8:21–58).

The Pharisees were denounced by Jesus for their outward morality but inward sinfulness, meticulous keeping of the minute aspects of the law while neglecting the greater matters of the law. Jesus denounced them for loving honor, desecrating people with their teaching, imposing burdensome extrabiblical regulations, spiritual blindness, and misinterpretation of Scripture (Luke 11:37–52). The Pharisees rejected the blind man's claim that Jesus had healed him and were enraged that Jesus healed on the Sabbath. They rejected Christ's claim to be the Good Shepherd and the Gate (John 9–10:21). The Pharisees attempted to stone and seize Jesus at the Feast of Dedication where Jesus claimed to be one with the Father as evidenced by His works (John 10:22–39).

The Pharisees were corrected and silenced by Jesus on their understanding of the Sabbath when Jesus showed them that it was lawful to help others, show mercy, and show compassion on the Sabbath (Luke 14:1–6). The Pharisees grumbled and scoffed at Jesus eating and welcoming sinners. Jesus would then give them three parables of how God seeks sinners, rejoices over repentant sinners, embraces repentant sinners, and gives full sonship and salvation to repentant sinners (Luke 15:1–32).

The Pharisees plotted to kill Jesus after He had raised Lazarus from the dead. They also plotted to kill Lazarus because many Jews were believing in Jesus (John 11:45–12:11). The Pharisees were given a parable by Jesus because they trusted in their own righteousness. Jesus illustrated the condemnation of self-righteousness and the justification of a tax collector who possessed repentant faith in God (Luke 18:9–14). The Pharisees were upset over the worship that Jesus was receiving during his entry into Jerusalem. Jesus affirmed and received the people's praise upon His entry into Jerusalem (Luke 19:28–44). The Pharisees intimated others from following Jesus by synagogue excommunication even though Jesus had done many signs to show that He was sent from the Father (John 12:37–50). The Pharisees continued their plot to kill Jesus after Jesus had cleansed the temple due to the false worship that was being offered in the name of the true God (Luke 19:45–48). The Pharisees sought to arrest Jesus when they realized Jesus told a parable about them which was a parable of them beating, stoning, and killing the prophets that God sent to them and even killing God's Son who was sent to them (Matthew 21:33–46).

The Pharisees tried to trap Jesus by asking Him a question on paying taxes to Caesar, but Jesus saw their hypocrisy and demonstrated that taxes should be paid to authorities established by God, but all worship and allegiance should be given to God. The Pharisees were left with no reply to Christ's divine answer (Matthew 22:15–22). A Pharisee, who was a scribe, asked Jesus what the greatest commandment was and Jesus gave a wise answer. The scribe replied back wisely and Jesus confirmed that the scribe was outside the kingdom, and no one dared asked Jesus another question (Mark 12:28–34).

The Pharisees were rebuked by Jesus for their hypocrisy, burdensome regulations, love of praise from men, publicly displaying their self-righteous deeds, love of honor, and refusal to be humbled (Matthew 23:1–12). The Pharisees would again be rebuked by Jesus for their hypocrisy for being false teachers who kept people out of the kingdom, for converting people to their damning religion, for their twisted system that allowed for lying and sinning, for paying attention to minor matters in the law rather than the weightier matters, for defiling themselves to the greatest extent by rejecting Him, for their outward morality but inward sin and spiritual deadness, and for their zeal and desire to crucify Him which was simply an indictment that they would have killed any prophet sent to them (Matthew 23:13–39).

THE GOSPEL CALL • 159

The chief priests and elders were responsible for the plot to arrest and kill Jesus (Matthew 26:1–5). The chief priests and scribes accepted Judas' proposal to betray Jesus (Luke 22:1–6). The chief priests, teachers of the law, and elders came to arrest Jesus which was a violation of their laws since they had no charge to bring against Him (Mark 14:43–52). The chief priests, teachers of the law, and elders held an unlawful and unjust trial at night that allowed for false evidence, false testimony, and false witnesses to try and find a reason to accuse and punish Jesus (Matthew 26: 57–67). The chief priests and teachers of the law accused Jesus in front of Herod for Jesus correctly saying that He was the Son of God and the Messiah (Luke 23:6–11). The chief priests and elders persuaded the crowd to release Barabbas rather than Jesus which ultimately resulted in the crucifixion of Jesus (Matthew 27:20–23). The Pharisees witnessed the miracles at Calvary which included the earthquake, the darkness, the splitting of the curtain in the temple, and tombs opening (Matthew 27:45, 51–53; Mark 15:33, 38).

This is all to say that there was an unbelievable amount of evidence that was performed by the Lord to show that He was the Christ, the Son of the Living God, and that there was salvation in Him alone. This is where we will transition to Nicodemus becoming the humble follower of Jesus.

John 19:38–40—*After these things Joseph of Arimathea, who was a disciple of Jesus, but secretly for fear of the Jews, asked Pilate that he might take away the body of Jesus, and Pilate gave him permission. So he came and took away his body. Nicodemus also, who earlier had come to Jesus by night, came bringing a mixture of myrrh and aloes, about seventy-five pounds in weight. So they took the body of Jesus and bound it in linen cloths with the spices, as it is the burial custom of the Jews.*

Nicodemus had witnessed much in the life of Christ. He needed to be humbled by the Lord in his understanding of regeneration, sin, righteousness, and salvation. Nicodemus had seen the Lord confront the false Judaism that was spread by the Pharisees. Nicodemus saw the willingness of Jesus to forgive sinners. He saw the miracles that were done, and he saw the divine teaching and wisdom from the Lord Jesus Christ. Nicodemus saw the miracles that happened at Calvary while Christ was suffering on the cross. Nicodemus saw that Jesus kept silent as a lamb led to the slaughter (Isaiah 53:7). Nicodemus saw the righteousness of Christ and the unrighteousness of the Pharisees. Ultimately, Nicodemus saw that the Son of Man was lifted up, just like Moses lifted up the serpent in the wilderness, so that those who would believe in Him would have eternal life (John 3:15). At some point, Nicodemus' heart of stone was made into a heart of flesh. At some point, the Spirt of God performed a miracle and caused Nicodemus to be born again. At some point, Nicodemus went from an unbeliever to a believer in the Lord Jesus Christ. This act of honor by Nicodemus was evidence of a regenerated, transformed, and redeemed life.

The resin the Nicodemus brought was a resin used to diminish the smell of decaying flesh. The aloes would serve the same purpose. Nicodemus brought 75 pounds which was a massive amount to show honor to a distinguished person. Nicodemus stepped out of the shadows and paid honor to Christ. By Nicodemus' actions, he had identified himself with Christ and he acknowledged the truth of what Christ taught and did. It is as if Nicodemus is saying, "I will honor Jesus and if you do to me what you did to Him, I accept it." Nicodemus is demonstrating the fruits of a submissive, preeminent loving, repentant, and humble faith in Christ. Nicodemus bore fruit of a self-denying, cross-bearing, self-hating, Christ-loving, Christ-following, repentant, and humble faith. That day, Nicodemus wrapped and handled the body of Jesus and laid Him in a tomb, not even knowing that he was fulfilling the prophecy of Isaiah 53. What a demonstration of mercy and compassion that Jesus came to save Nicodemus who was a false-teaching Pharisee. What a demonstration of love that Jesus drew Nicodemus to Himself in salvation. What a Savior who forgives false teachers and makes them His prized possession.

There is tradition that says that Nicodemus was baptized by Peter and John and that his devotion to Christ cost him his position as a teacher and being a member of the Sanhedrin. The tradition says that Nicodemus lost his fortune, property, possessions and was relegated to living in absolute poverty. A man named Photius refers to an ancient document that records that Nicodemus was martyred in the first century for his devotion to Christ by being beaten to death by a mob. Nicodemus was one that lost his life to save it. Nicodemus was one who understood Christ's teaching that it profits a man nothing if he gains the whole world yet forfeits his soul. Nicodemus was a sheep of the Good Shepherd. Nicodemus would have Christ's resonating, eternal, and comforting words where Jesus said this in Luke 12:32, "Fear not, little flock, for it is your Father's good pleasure to give you the kingdom." The honored Jewish Pharisee had become the humbled Jesus follower. As we close chapter 5, let us reflect on James' call to humble yourself before the Lord and the promise of His exaltation for those that will be humbled. James, the half-brother of Jesus would have surely known of Nicodemus' act of honoring Jesus as the apostle John captured this act in his gospel and was an esteemed pillar in the Jerusalem church along with James.

Jesus can save the most ritualistic, ceremonial, sacramental, and religious false teacher or church member. The same Son that hardens the dirt is the same Son that can melt snow. Jesus Christ is powerful to save. Salvation is from the Lord and belongs to the Lord (Psalm 3:8).

CHAPTER 6

James: Let Not Many Become Teachers

James 3:1—*Let not many of you become teachers, my brethren, knowing that as such we will incur a stricter judgment.*

James gives a very simple instruction that those who would profess to be Christians should approach such a decision to become a teacher with utmost cautiousness. Although it is noble to desire being a teacher, this is a decision that must be made with care, fear, caution, prayer, and diligence. James has strong reason for giving such a command to those professing Christ as Lord and Savior.

The Danger of False Teaching
The first reason for James' warning comes from biblical history. The history of Israel is one which shows the devastation that was brought on by teachers who would not teach God's truth and were false teachers. James certainly saw this devastation with the Pharisees and Sadducees, but the history of damning false teachers is a constant threat in the Old Testament as well. Jeremiah records such accounts of prophets and teachers speaking falsely. In Jeremiah 5:12–13 it says "They have spoken falsely of the LORD

and have said, 'He will do nothing; no disaster will come upon us, nor shall we see sword or famine. The prophets will become wind; the word is not in them. Thus shall it be done to them!'" Here, we see that the LORD was angry with the false prophets who stood in the place of true prophets and spoke falsely in the name of the LORD. Thus, the false prophets would be treated as guilty for their treachery.

In Jeremiah 5:30–31 it says this regarding the false prophets, "An appalling and horrible thing has happened in the land: the prophets prophesy falsely, and the priests rule at their direction; my people love to have it so, but what will you do when the end comes?" The LORD is essentially saying that the prophets are speaking falsely but pretending to speak for the LORD. Likewise, the priests ruled in the same manner. The prophets did not speak God's Word and the priests did not do God's work. The LORD asks a very simple question, "What will you do when the end comes?" The undeniable answer is that when one prophesies falsely and rule with their own self-will and lead people astray, the end for the prophet and the people will be disastrous.

In Jeremiah 6:13–15, the LORD says this regarding false prophets, "'For from the least to the greatest of them, everyone is greedy for unjust gain; and from prophet to priest, everyone deals falsely. They have healed the wound of my people lightly, saying, 'Peace, peace,' when there is no peace. Were they ashamed when they committed abomination? No, they were not at all ashamed; they did not know how to blush. Therefore they shall fall among those who fall; at the time that I punish them, they shall be overthrown,' says the Lord." The false prophets and false teachers did not deal seriously with the spiritual wound of sin and its effects. Instead of warning the people and turning them from sin, they told the people that there was peace with God when there was no peace. What is most striking is that we could see the false prophets were not ashamed. The false prophets couldn't even blush.

The false prophets did not even know how to be ashamed for leading their people astray.

In Jeremiah 8:10–12, the prophet makes a similar statement where he says, "Therefore I will give their wives to others and their fields to conquerors, because from the least to the greatest everyone is greedy for unjust gain; from prophet to priest, everyone deals falsely. They have healed the wound of my people lightly, saying, 'Peace, peace,' when there is no peace. Were they ashamed when they committed abomination? No, they were not at all ashamed; they did not know how to blush. Therefore they shall fall among the fallen; when I punish them, they shall be overthrown, says the LORD." Once again, the false teachers weren't being condemned for just minor errors in teaching. No, they were condemned for treating sin lightly and prophesying peace with God when there is no peace. They were preaching a false message of reconciliation with the LORD when there was no reconciliation. We see in this verse as well that the false prophets were not even ashamed of leading people astray. They did not even know how to blush. False prophets and teachers had no shame, no sorrow, no sadness over the spiritual destruction they were a part of and leading others into.

In Jeremiah 23:16–17, the LORD says, "Thus says the LORD of hosts: 'Do not listen to the words of the prophets who prophesy to you, filling you with vain hopes. They speak visions of their own minds, not from the mouth of the LORD. They say continually to those who despise the word of the LORD, "It shall be well with you"; and to everyone who stubbornly follows his own heart, they say, 'No disaster shall come upon you.'" Here, again, you have false prophets who give false hopes and claim that all will be well with the LORD's people when it is not well. The false prophets are not making some minor doctrinal error, but rather, they are knowingly giving a message of peace and comfort when there really should be a message of warning and judgment. The false teachers and false prophets do not have a message of reconciliation. The false prophets will not repent. They just continue to lead their followers to disaster.

In Jeremiah 23:25–32, the LORD says, "I have heard what the prophets have said who prophesy lies in my name, saying, 'I have dreamed, I have dreamed!' How long shall there be lies in the heart of the prophets who prophesy lies, and who prophesy the deceit of their own heart, who think to make my people forget my name by their dreams that they tell one another, even as their fathers forgot my name for Baal? Let the prophet who has a dream tell the dream, but let him who has my word speak my word faithfully. What has straw in common with wheat? declares the Lord. Is not my word like fire, declares the Lord, and like a hammer that breaks the rock in pieces? Therefore, behold, I am against the prophets, declares the Lord, who steal my words from one another. Behold, I am against the prophets, declares the Lord, who use their tongues and declare, 'declares the Lord.' Behold, I am against those who prophesy lying dreams, declares the Lord, and who tell them and lead my people astray by their lies and their recklessness, when I did not send them or charge them. So they do not profit this people at all, declares the Lord." The LORD is angry over false teachers and false prophets who stand up and act as though they are speaking for the Lord when they are really not. In fact, the LORD promises that those who would teach falsely will be cast away from His presence, bear an everlasting reproach, and everlasting perpetual shame that will never be forgotten (Jeremiah 23:39–40).

In Ezekiel 13:9–12, the LORD speaks against the false prophets through Ezekiel where He says, "My hand will be against the prophets who see false visions and who give lying divinations. They shall not be in the council of my people, nor be enrolled in the register of the house of Israel, nor shall they enter the land of Israel. And you shall know that I am the LORD God. Precisely because they have misled my people saying, 'Peace, when there is no peace,' and because when the people build a wall, these prophets smear it with whitewash, say to those who smear it with whitewash that it shall fall! There will be a deluge of rain, and you, O great hailstones, will fall, and a stormy wind break out. And when the wall falls, will it not be said to you, 'Where is the coating with which you smeared it?'" The false prophets had lulled the people into false security. They gave phony "peace" promises while sin continued on the brink of God's judgment. They essentially erected a defective "wall" and whitewashed it to make it look good. Such an unsafe "wall" was doomed to collapse when God would bring His storm, or rather, when Israel would be invaded. The false teachers led the people astray, promised peace when God was angry with them, and continually and superficially addressed Israel's sin problem. In Ezekiel 13:16, He says, "Those prophets of Israel who prophesied to Jerusalem saw visions of peace for her when there was no peace, declares the Sovereign LORD." What a horrible and abominable thing it is to stand as God's representative and declare peace to God's people when there is no peace with God!

Jesus spoke much about false teachers and false prophets. Jesus warned that there would be false prophets that looked like true teachers (Matthew 7:15-20). Jesus warned of the dangerous influence of false teachers and their teaching (Matthew 16:5-12, Mark 12:38-40). James would have known about Christ denouncing false teachers (Luke 11:37-54, Matthew 23:1-36, Matthew 15:1-20, Luke 16:14-15). James would know that false teachers would receive a greater condemnation (Mark 12:40). James saw that false teaching and false gospels were being propagated in the early church (James 15:1-13). This is all to say that James had a strong reason to command professing Christians not to be many teachers.

Thus, it is clear that James was aware of the deception and destruction that false prophets and false teachers had on a nation. To stand as a representative for the Lord and lead people away from Him through one's teaching or one's life would be absolutely disastrous.

For those in the Eastern Orthodox Church, Oriental Orthodox Church, Greek Orthodox Church, Assyrian Orthodox Church, Lutheran Church, Anglican Church denominations, United Methodist Churches, United Church of Christ or any other church that would teach regeneration, conversion, or salvation through sacraments has been thoroughly deceived. Such a teacher needs to repent and humble themselves before the Lord.

There is more that could be explained on false teachers, but the following is a helpful definition of a false teacher: **A false teacher is one who holds to, unrepentantly, and persistently teaches and preaches a false gospel that damns men's souls by attacking, twisting, misinterpreting, adding to, or leaving out the essential components of the gospel or essential components of the bad news of sin, death, and hell. A false teacher could also be one who teaches the true gospel but lives a life in contradiction and opposition to the gospel and thus, blasphemes the gospel through their life** (Galatians 1:6–9, Matthew 15:14, 23:13–15; 2 Peter 2:1–22, 3:16; Luke 11:52; Jude 4).

Desire for Honor, Prestige, and the Praise of Men

We see that Jesus spoke about the danger a teacher could face when it came to being revered and honored by men. Jesus said this of the Pharisees in Matthew 23:5-7, "They do all their deeds to be seen by others. For they make their phylacteries broad and their fringes long, and they love the place of honor at feasts and the best seats in the synagogues and greetings in the marketplaces and being called rabbi by others." There is certainly a temptation that comes with being a teacher and in a position of leadership. Jesus called His disciples to serve others and love one another (John 13:1-17, 13:33-35). One who loves honor, prestige, and praise of men is not one who will serve others and give of himself self-sacrificially. Therefore, those who exhibit a proclivity toward loving honor, prestige, and the praise of men are not those who should serve as a pastor or elder.

Qualifications and Responsibilities of an Elder or Pastor

In Paul's epistles, he lists out many qualifications and duties for an elder. Such qualifications would include being above reproach, or rather, free from open accusation (1 Timothy 3:1). The elder must be faithful to one's wife (1 Timothy 3:2). The elder must be sober-minded, self-controlled, respectable, hospitable, able to teach, not a drunkard, not violent but gentle, not quarrelsome, not a lover of money (1 Timothy 3:2-3). The elder must be able to manage his household well and with honor (1 Timothy 3:5). The elder must not be a recent convert so he is not puffed up and conceited (1 Timothy 3:6). The elder must have a good reputation with those outside the church (1 Timothy 3:7). The elder must avoid myths and train himself in righteousness and godliness (1 Timothy 4:7). The elder must set an example in speech, conduct, love, faith and purity (1 Timothy 4:12). The elder must be devoted to the teaching of Scripture (1 Timothy 4:13). The elder must carefully watch over his teaching and manner of life (1 Timothy 4:16). An elder must be able to rebuke unrepentant sinners (1 Timothy 5:21). An elder must be discerning on the commissioning of other pastors and elders (1 Timothy 5:22). An elder is called to be content with what he has been given by the Lord (1 Timothy 6:6-8). An elder is to pursue righteousness, godliness, faith, love, steadfastness, and gentleness (1 Timothy 6:11). An elder is called to rightly handle the Word of truth (2 Timothy 2:15). An elder is called to be able to instruct opponents (2 Timothy 2:24-26). An elder is called to preach the Word (1 Timothy 4:1-5). An elder must endure difficulty and apostasy (2 Timothy 3:1-9). An elder must be able to give sound instruction and refute those who contradict sound doctrine (Titus 1:9). An elder must not devote themselves and have nothing to do with myths, endless genealogies, irreverent myths, silly myths, irreverent babble, foolish controversies, ignorant controversies, Jewish myths, dissensions, quarrels about the law (1 Timothy 1:4, 4:7, 6:20, 2 Timothy 2:23, Titus 1:14, 3:9). An elder must not be quick tempered (Titus 1:7). An elder must be a lover of strangers and hospitable (Titus 1:8). An elder must be able to sharply rebuke false teachers (Titus 1:13).

The previous paragraph lists the qualifications and responsibilities of an elder or pastor. However, we could list all of these qualifications and responsibilities in a negative sense. For example, a man that is not above reproach or is open to accusation would not be qualified to be a pastor or elder (1 Timothy 3:1). Such reproach could be an argumentative spirit, preoccupation with money and materialism, a tendency to show strong favoritism toward church members, and could include several other areas of one's life. A man that is flirtatious, adulterous, a fornicator, or addicted to pornography would not be qualified as a pastor or elder (1 Timothy 3:2). A man with a dysfunctional family and who is not able to provide good leadership in his family would not be qualified as a pastor or elder (1 Timothy 3:5). A man that is a new convert and is even gifted in teaching would not be qualified as an elder or pastor because of the risk of falling into pride (1 Timothy 3:6). A man who is not devoted to learning and teaching Scripture would not be qualified as a pastor or elder (1 Timothy 4:13). Such a man may be one who likes to perform pastoral visits, set up and prepare for church events, lead a music ministry, but spends little or no time studying God's Word. Such a man would not be qualified as a pastor or elder. A man who is not willing to confront sin and false teachers would not be qualified to be an elder or pastor (1 Timothy 5:21, Titus 1:9). Such a man that will not rebuke false teachers or unrepentant sinners will eventually lead people astray from the gospel and the truth of God's Word. A man who will not preach God's Word is unqualified to be an elder or pastor (1 Timothy 4:2). Such a man could be a man that talks about human philosophy, social justice, social issues, psychology, world issues, and uses God's Word only as a medium to discuss other subjects. A man who cannot rightly handle God's Word would not be qualified to be a pastor or elder (2 Timothy 2:15). Such a man may have a faulty view in Christology, soteriology, systematic theology, hamartiology, pneumatology, anthropology, bibliology, ecclesiology, or eschatology. If a man is not able to rightly handle God's Word, he is unfit to be a pastor or elder. As we can clearly see, pastors or elders are called to carry out these commands as ambassadors and representatives of Christ. The role of a teacher is serious and should never be taken lightly. This position is the most noble task that one could seek, but it is also the most dangerous of tasks as it invites the stricter judgment of the Lord (James 3:1).

A Condemnation of Sacramental Conversion

As we went through James' gospel invitation to come to the Lord Jesus Christ in saving faith, it should become blatantly clear that true conversion is eternities apart from sacramental conversion. Sacramental conversion in any form is a false message and a false gospel of reconciliation. Sacramental conversion is taught in Eastern Orthodox Church, Oriental Orthodox Church, Greek Orthodox Church, Assyrian Orthodox Church, Lutheran Church, Anglican Church denominations, United Methodist Churches, United Church of Christ, and more. This would include baptism, chrismation, taking communion, confirmation, marriage, or any other ritual or ceremony. For one to put their hope and assurance of salvation in any sacrament, ritual, or ceremony is disastrous and damning. Likewise, for those that would say that becoming a Christian is simply head knowledge of the facts of the gospel have been deceived.

Jesus would give strong warnings to those who would lead people astray and preach or teach a false gospel. In Matthew 18:6, Jesus gives this warning about causing someone who believes in

Him to sin, "but whoever causes one of these little ones who believe in me to stumble, it would be better for him to have a great millstone fastened around his neck and to be drowned in the depth of the sea." In other words, if a false teacher would teach that one is born again, converted, and saved because of going through or partaking in some sacrament, it would be better for that false teacher to suffer a violent and horrific death than to cause a believer in Christ to stumble. How much more severe would it be to try and convince a Christian or even an unbeliever that one is saved through sacraments?

Jesus was both compassionate and confrontational with false teachers. Jesus gave the false teachers the truth, but never backed down when the truth was being attacked. Jesus warned that false teachers were ravenous wolves (Matthew 7:15). Jesus warned that false teachers would bear bad fruit, or rather, bad doctrinal fruit or bad moral and lifestyle fruit (Matthew 7:16-20). Jesus warned that false teachers would be cut down and thrown into hell (Matthew 7:20). Jesus called false teachers hypocrites (Matthew 15:7). Jesus would proclaim that false teachers worshiped God in vain (Matthew 15:9). Jesus proclaimed that false teachers are blind guides (Matthew 15:14). Jesus commanded that unrepentant false teachers should be left alone and avoided (Matthew 15:14). Jesus commanded His followers to beware of the permeating influence and danger of false teachers (Matthew 16:5-12). Jesus denounced false teachers for shutting the kingdom of heaven in men's faces, or rather, keeping people out of the kingdom of heaven through their false teaching (Matthew 23:13). Jesus denounced false teachers who damned the people that came under their teaching and influence (Matthew 23:15). Jesus called false teachers children of hell (Matthew 23:15). Jesus called false teachers blind fools (Matthew 23:17). Jesus called false teachers blind (Matthew 23:26). Jesus denounced false teachers for their outward morality but inward corruption and remaining unregenerate and unconverted on the inside

(Matthew 23:25-28). Jesus called false teachers serpents and a brood of vipers (Matthew 23:33). Jesus denounced false teachers for their love of honor (Luke 11:43). Jesus denounced false teachers because their teaching defiled those who came under its influence (Luke 11:44). Jesus denounced false teachers for misinterpreting Scripture to such an extent that it kept people out of the kingdom of heaven (Luke 11:52). Jesus warned of false teachers being hypocrites, or rather, those that would stand as a true teacher of the Lord but were false teachers that damned men's souls (Luke 12:1). Jesus was very concerned about false teachers who would stand as true teachers but would ultimately damn men's souls through their false teaching or false gospels.

Paul gave strong warnings to those who would lead people astray and preach or teach a false gospel. Paul would issue this warning in Galatians 1:8-9 about anyone who would unrepentantly teach or preach a false gospel, "But even if we or an angel from heaven should preach to you a gospel contrary to the one we preached to you, let him be accursed. As we have said before, so now I say again: If anyone is preaching to you a gospel contrary to the one you received, let him be accursed." Paul pronounced fiery condemnation on those who would preach a false gospel. Such a person who would preach a false gospel was to be damned by God. Such a person who preached a false gospel was a gospel perverter, a gospel distorter, a gospel corrupter, and an outright enemy of the gospel (Galatians 1:7). To claim that one is saved by sacraments it to proclaim that Christ died for nothing according to Paul (Galatians 2:21). To proclaim that one can be saved through sacraments is to put yourself and those under you under God's curse (Galatians 3:10, 13). To proclaim that one can be saved through sacraments is to make someone obligated to keep the whole law, and thus, damn someone's soul (Galatians 3:10, 13). To proclaim that one can be saved through sacraments is to make Christ's salvific work of no benefit (Galatians 5:2). To proclaim that one can be saved through sacraments is to sever and completely cut people off from Christ (Galatians 5:3-4). To proclaim that one can be saved through sacraments is to make false converts into full fledged pagans (Galatians 5:12).

Paul took false teachers very seriously. Paul knew that eternity was at stake, and he dealt with them with great gravity and urgency. Paul warned that false teachers would come from outside the church and within the church (Acts 20:29-30). Paul gave a command that false teachers should be rebuked and commanded to stop false teaching (1 Timothy 1:3-5, Titus 1:9, 1:11). Paul commanded that false teachers be rebuked sharply (Titus 1:13). Paul commanded that false teachers should be warned and then shunned (Titus 3:9). Paul commanded that false teachers should be instructed and taught if possible (Titus 1:9, 2 Timothy 2:24-26). Paul commanded that believers were to turn away from false teachers (Romans 16:17). Paul commanded that unrepentant false teachers were to be shunned (2 Timothy 3:5).

Peter gave strong warnings to those who would lead people astray and preach or teach a false gospel. Peter wrote that a false teacher who would introduce destructive heresies and blaspheme the way of truth was to be under God's condemnation (2 Peter 2:1-3). Peter declared that false teachers were subjects of God's wrath (2 Peter 2:4-10). Peter proclaimed that false teachers were nothing more than irrational animals of instinct that were born to be caught and destroyed (2 Peter 2:12). Peter declares that false teachers had forsaken the right way and had gone astray (2 Peter 2:15). Peter declared that gloom and utter darkness had been reserved for them (2 Peter 2:17). Peter declares that false teachers promise freedom, but provide no such freedom (2 Peter 2:19). Peter states that those false teachers who have been given the truth but refuse to repent would be better off having never been told the truth as their condemnation will be greater (2 Peter 2:20-22, Luke 12:47). Peter warned that false teachers would twist Scripture to their own destruction (2 Peter 3:16). Peter warned that false teachers would be ignorant and unstable

(2 Peter 3:16). Peter warned believers to not be carried away and influenced by false teachers (2 Peter 3:17).

The apostle John gave strong warnings to those who would lead people astray and false teach as well. John warned that believers were to test doctrine to determine whether a teacher was true or false as there were many false prophets that had gone into the world (1 John 4:1). John explained that teachers who had a false Christology were false teachers and antichrists (1 John 4:2-3). John warned that false teachers would give a message that was in some way, shape or form, friendly to the world as the world would listen to them (1 John 4:5). John proclaimed that many deceivers and false teachers had gone out into the world (2 John 7). John warned that false teachers would not abide in the teaching of Christ and go beyond what Christ taught (2 John 9). John proclaimed that such a person that went beyond the teaching of Christ was one who did not have God which means they were damned and taught a false gospel (2 John 9). John commanded that false teachers should not be given a Christian greeting (2 John 10). John commanded that false teachers should not be welcomed into one's house or supported (2 John 10). John warned that one who greeted a false teacher or provided support was guilty of fellowshipping and partaking in the wicked works of a false teacher (2 John 11).

Teaching sacramental conversion and salvation amounts to a false gospel. Teaching sacramental conversion and salvation amounts to a works-salvation (Galatians 2:21). Teaching sacramental conversion and salvation is a false gospel and really is no gospel at all (Galatians 1:6-7). Teaching sacramental conversion and salvation is to be accursed (Galatians 1:8-9). Teaching sacramental conversion and salvation is to teach a perverted and corrupted false gospel (Galatians 1:7). Teaching sacramental conversion and salvation is a destructive heresy (2 Peter 2:1). Teaching sacramental conversion and salvation is to twist Scripture to one's own destruction (2 Peter 3:16).

Let us learn from James, the half-brother of Jesus, on what true conversion unto the Lord Jesus Christ is. Let us learn from Jesus, John, Paul, the New Testament writers, and the Holy Spirit on the dangers of false teaching, the responsibility of pastors and elders, and that teachers and preachers are subject to the stricter judgment. Let us learn that Jesus is the Way, the Truth, and the Life and that no one comes to the Father except through Him (John 14:6). Let us learn from James and Jesus that the response to the gospel was one of repentance and faith in the Lord Jesus Christ. Let us learn from James and Jesus that the saving faith or faith that justifies is a submissive, meek, loving, repentant, and humble faith in the Lord Jesus Christ (James 4:7–10; Matthew 4:17, 5:3–6, 16:24–26; Mark 1:15, 8:34–37; Luke 3:3–17, 9:23–26, 13:1–5, 14:25–33; John 12:24–26).

All praise and honor be given for the glory of God and the building up of Christ's church. Amen.

"Father, have mercy on the blind and hard-hearted in sacramental churches. Open their eyes that they may see the truth of Your gospel, repent, and be saved. Do this all for Your glory. Amen."

Author Definitions

Sin: is breaking God's law by either not doing what God's law demands (James 4:17) or doing what God's law prohibits (James 2:10) by any thought (Matthew 5:28), word (Matthew 5:22), deed (Matthew 5:39), or intent (Matthew 6:1) which God hates (Psalm 5:5, 11:5), abhors (Psalm 5:6), is angered with (Psalm 7:11), is ready to destroy and punish (Psalm 7:12-13), which is being at warfare with Him (James 4:4), which God considers an abomination (Proverbs 22:12), and which God considers evil (Psalm 7:9).

Hell: is a place of God's full wrath and is a place of blackest darkness (Jude 13, Matthew 22:13), filled with furious and concentrated fire everywhere (Matthew 5:22, 5:29, 13:42, 13:50), where there is weeping and anger against God for the unrepentant Christ-rejecting (Matthew 11:20-24) and Christ-neglecting sinners (Hebrews 2:1-3) where they will spend all eternity paying for every sin they've ever committed (Revelation 20:12) with no hope of escape (Luke 16:26), and only the expectation of excruciating torments to their body, soul, and spirit (Matthew 10:28) and an undying conscience that will haunt them day and night, forever and ever, with no reprieve (Luke 16:25).

Person of the Lord Jesus Christ: is the Jewish Messiah and Son of the Living God (Matthew 16:16, Romans 1:1-4). Jesus is God and He is coequal and coeternal with God the Father and God the Holy Spirit (John 5:17-18, 10:30, 10:38, 14:10). Jesus is the eternal, only begotten, one-of-a-kind, Son of God (John 3:16). Jesus is the Anointed One of God (Luke 4:18-19). Jesus is the Savior of the world (Luke 2:11). Jesus is the Creator and Sustainer of the Universe (John 1:1-14). Jesus is the Son of David (Matthew 1:1-16, Luke 3:23-38). Jesus was born of a virgin (Matthew 1:23, Galatians 4:4). Jesus was the Word made flesh (John 1:14). Jesus was physically born into this world as a man (Matthew 1:25). Jesus is thus truly God and truly man (Philippians 2:5-11).

Work of the Lord Jesus Christ: is Jesus lived a sinless life (Matthew 26:59-60, 1 Corinthians 5:21) and fulfilled all righteousness found in the law and prophets (Matthew 5:17-20, Luke 24:44-46). He declared Himself to be the Christ (Matthew 16:16), the only begotten Son of the Living God through His teaching (John 3:16, Matthew 22:41-46), which was attested to by His miracles and display of divine power (John 10:37-38). Jesus offered himself as a spotless and blameless sacrifice for sin (John 1:29) to propitiate the righteous anger of God by taking all the sins of God's people (John 10:11, Romans 3:25, Isaiah 53) and, thus, the full wrath of God that was due to man (Matthew 26:39, 27:45-46, Luke 22:44). His sacrifice propitiated the righteous anger of God and reconciled (Romans 5:10-11) and brought peace from man to God and God to man (Matthew 27:51-53, John 19:30, Romans 5:1). His substitutionary sacrifice and death also redeemed sinful man to Holy God by forgiving man's sin (Hebrews 8:12, Ephesians 1:7) and imputing Christ's righteousness to man (1 Corinthians 5:21, Isaiah 53:1-12, Romans 4:3-5). Jesus was resurrected from the dead on the third day by His own power (John 10:18), by God the Father (Galatians 1:1) and God the Holy Spirit (Romans 8:11), which affirmed His person, His teachings, and salvific work for sinners (Romans 4:25). He ascended to the right hand of the Father (Luke 24:51) and is empowered with all authority to bring about the plan of salvation for all His people (Matthew 28:18) by causing them to be born again (John 3:1-10) and justified by His grace (John 3:16, 3:18, 3:36). He will also return to bring all His own to heaven with Him (John 6:37-40, 14:1-3) to be glorified (John 17:24) while also judging and condemning Satan, demons, and sinful man (Matthew 25:31-46, Revelation 20:7-15)

Baptism of the Holy Spirit: Is the sovereign monergistic work of salvation performed by God the Father, God the Son, and God the Holy Spirit. The Holy Spirit is given from the Father to the Son (John 14:16, 15:26, Luke 11:13) and the Son pours out or gives the Holy Spirit in the Father's name (Matthew 3:11- 12, Mark 1:8, Luke 3:16, 24:49 John 1:31-33, 14:16, 14:26, 15:26, 16:7; Acts 1:4-5, 2:17-18, 10:44-48, 11:16, Titus 3:6). The Holy Spirit then regenerates or causes man to be born again (John 3:3-10, Titus 3:5, Ezekiel 36:25-27) through hearing the Word of God/Gospel (James 1:18, Ephesians 1:13, Romans 1:15- 17, 10:17, 1 Corinthians 1 21) which gives spiritual life to the previously spiritually dead man (Ephesians 2:1-3, Colossians 2:13). God then grants man the ability to repent which is a gift (Acts 11:18, 2 Timothy 2:25) and put saving faith in Jesus Christ which is also a gift (Ephesians 2:8-9, Philippians 1:29, John 7:38-39). Man is then justified by grace through faith in Christ (Titus 3:7), receives and is indwelt by the Holy Spirit (Galatians 3:2, 3:14, Ephesians 1:13, 1 Corinthians 6:19), and the Holy Spirit spiritually unites/immerses man with Jesus Christ and puts the man into the body of Christ (1 Corinthians 12:13, Romans 6:3-4). The baptism with the Holy Spirit is not water baptism and water baptism is not the baptism with the Holy Spirit for only Christ can baptize with the Holy Spirit and man can only baptize with water (Matthew 3:11-12, Mark 1:8, Luke 3:16, John 1:31-33, 3:8, 7:38-39, 14:15-17, 14:26, 15:26, 16:7; Acts 1:4-5, 2:17-18, 10:44-48, 11:16, 1 Corinthians 1:17). The baptism with the Holy Spirit is a one-time, instantaneous, and salvific work of God (1 Corinthians 12:13).

Regeneration: Is the sovereign monergistic work of God the Holy Spirit in giving spiritual life (Ezekiel 36:24-27, 11:19-20, Jeremiah 24:7, 31:31-34, 32:38-40, John 3:1-10, Titus 3:5-6) to spiritually dead (Ephesians 2:1-5, Colossians 1:21) and sinful man through hearing the Word of God/Gospel (James 1:18, Ephesians 1:13, Romans 1:15- 17, 10:17, 1 Corinthians 1:21) so that man is enabled, gifted, and granted to repent (Acts 5:31, 11:18, 2 Timothy 2:25) and enabled, gifted, and granted to respond in saving faith to Jesus Christ (Ephesians 2:8-9, Philippians

1:29, Hebrews 12:2). Regeneration also known as being born again and the new birth (John 3:3-10, 1 Peter 1:3, 1:23)

Repentance: is a gift from God (Acts 5:31, 11:18, 2 Timothy 2:25) where the sinner understands his sin against God and is poor in spirit (Matthew 5:3, Luke 18:9-14), has godly sorrow and mourns over his sin against God (Matthew 5:4, 2 Corinthians 7:10), and turns away from his sin and toward God for righteousness and salvation (Matthew 5:5-6, Luke 3:3-17, Acts 17:30, 20:21, 1 Thessalonians 1:9).

Saving Faith: is a gift from God (Ephesians 2:8-9) where a sinner has knowledge of Jesus' person and work where a sinner will respond to Christ's person and work by denying themselves (Matthew 16:24, Mark 8:34, Luke 9:23), picking up their cross (Matthew 10:38, 16:24, Mark 8:34, Luke 9:23), and lovingly (Luke 14:26-27, James 4:7) and obediently (2 Thessalonians 1:8, Romans 1:5) submitting (James 4:6, Matthew 11:28) and committing their life (Matthew 10:37-39, 16:24-26, Mark 8:34-37, Luke 9:23-26, 14:25-33) to Jesus and trusting in Him only for salvation (Romans 10:13, John 3:16, John 3:36, Acts 4:12).

Conversion: is the spiritual turning away from sin in repentance and to the Lord Jesus Christ in faith (Acts 20:21, 1 Thessalonians 1:9, Ephesians 4:22-24, Colossians 3:9-10, Mark 1:15)

Bibliography

Edersheim, Alfred. *The Life and Times of Jesus the Messiah.* London: Longmans, Green Co., 1923.

Lawson, Steve. "Blessed Bankruptcy, Part 2" (sermon), March 29, 2009.

Lawson, Steve. "Good Grief" (sermon), June April 19, 2009.

www.ingramcontent.com/pod-product-compliance
Lightning Source LLC
Chambersburg PA
CBHW061944070426
42450CB00007BA/1042